Whisky in Your Pocket

Wallace Milroy
and
Neil Wilson

WAVERLEY BOOKS

Published 2010 by Waverley Books, 144 Port Dundas Road,
Glasgow, G4 0HZ, Scotland

Excepting pages 61, 80, 95, 110, 116, 136, 170, 177,
180 (lower), 184 (lower), 186 (lower) all bottle and
packaging illustrations are reproduced by kind permission
of the online whisky shop www.masterofmalt.com.

The publisher accepts no responsibility whatsoever for the
accuracy of the bottle illustrations that appear in this book
which have been reproduced in good faith in the best effort
to represent the most up-to-date images.

Graphics on pages 7-16 are by Doreen Shaw.
www.theillustrator.co.uk

All maps are by Robert and Rhoda Burns/Drawing Attention.

ISBN 978-1-84934-023-6

Printed and bound in Poland

Contents

Introduction

IT is 12 years since the last edition of my *Malt Whisky Almanac* was published. First launched in 1986 the almanac evolved through seven editions and reached 300,000 sales with foreign editions also published in Japan, USA, Canada, Germany and Italy. Many people have asked me why an eighth edition never materialised but after it had sold out I felt that it had served its purpose in introducing whisky drinkers to the world of malt whisky and that it was time to let it rest for a while.

In the intervening years the market for single malts has expanded every year and in particular the BRIC nations (Brazil, Russia, India and China) have created huge demand from a largely aspirational and wealthy group of people who regard single malt Scotch whisky as a status symbol. However, the newcomers to the world of Scotch whisky who are hungry to start investigating feel overwhelmed with the amount of product and information in front of them. Even the issue of 'who owns what' is an eye-opener.

I often see a lot of confused consumers in the spirits' section of my local supermarket, staring at the malts and blends with next to nothing to help them make an informed choice. This, along with the increasing number of single malt bottlings being issued by the distillers means there is a demand for a return to first principles and to once again engage the curious consumer with the basic whisky facts and tasting notes for the single malt category, along with the other categories of Scotch. I was therefore delighted when my publisher and fellow co-writer Neil Wilson, who had been thinking along the same lines, approached me with a proposal to relaunch the almanac which we have now done with Waverley Books of Glasgow.

We are not decrying the mass of information that is out there, we are simply keen that the newcomer to whisky gets the correct information in as simple a fashion as

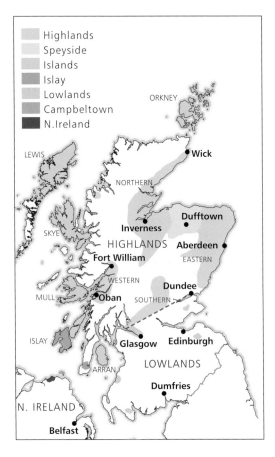

Highlands
Speyside
Islands
Islay
Lowlands
Campbeltown
N.Ireland

ORKNEY

LEWIS

Wick

NORTHERN

SKYE

Dufftown
Inverness

HIGHLANDS Aberdeen

Fort William

EASTERN

WESTERN

Dundee

MULL Oban SOUTHERN

ISLAY

Glasgow Edinburgh

LOWLANDS

ARRAN

Dumfries

N. IRELAND

Belfast

possible. *Whisky in Your Pocket* is the result of this approach and we hope it fulfils your requirements, particularly if you are a beginner.

In order to present the world of Scotch (and Northern Irish) whisk(e)y in a simple manner in this book, the producing regions are presented with Speyside first, then the Highland region in four areas (Eastern, Northern, Southern, Western) followed by the Lowlands, Islay, Campbeltown, the Islands and finally Northern Ireland. Within these regions there are some new single malts to welcome such as Kilchoman on Islay as well as some other enterprises at differing ends of the commercial spectrum; the tiny Loch Ewe Distillery operating next to the Drumchork Lodge Hotel at Aultbea in Wester Ross is a long way from the new Lowland malt distillery, Ailsa Bay, within William Grant's Girvan grain-distilling complex with an annual capacity of five million litres of alcohol.

In a similar vein, the variety and shelf presence of many malt bottlings is determined by the availability of vintages and the wood management policies of distillers as to how they wish to complete the maturation process of these whiskies. Some distillers use an increasingly varied range of wood types such as calvados, madeira, red wine, champagne, rum and port (to name just a few) in which they 'finish' off their malts for a short period of time. However, the relatively low outturn of these expressions means that they are not going to be found in supermarkets and this is one of the reasons why we have only detailed the core UK trade bottling for each of the brands featured. Anyone wanting to explore beyond this can simply search the relevant producer's website and then purchase from specialist retailers or online whisky shops.

The tasting notes used in this book are those of the proprietors where available (or the independent bottler) and describe the whisky after water has been added, unless stated. Any set of notes is subjective, but these are here to help, not to hinder, and have been rendered as simply as possible. The addition of water is to your taste but some malts do not require them and can be treated like a fine cognac or armagnac after dinner. All cask-strength single malts and single grains should have some water added (bit by bit if need be … you can always add water but never take it away!) but that is not to say you should not taste a small amount at full strength first.

Diageo owns the largest number of active distilleries (28) along with many malts from distilleries that are defunct or no longer exist. Their core malt brands such as Cardhu, Lagavulin and Talisker are readily available but malts from lost distilleries such as Port Ellen and Coleburn are released in limited quantities on a year-by-year basis if available. Until 2005 many of these were released as part of the Rare Malts Selection but since then they have been included in their annual Special Releases series. Due to their very nature these differ from year to year and in this guide we have tried to detail the most recent releases although some of the discontinued Rare Malts bottlings are still available from specialist retailers. They also issued another series branded 'Flora and Fauna' (reflecting each distillery's unique locality) but these have now been subsumed into their Distillery Malts series. Finally they also have a Manager's Choice which appears from time to time. All of these can be accessed at www.malts.com. Some of these rare whiskies may be much more expensive than other expressions from the same distillery, but don't be put off by high price points as many of the specialist retailers will hold stocks from independent bottlers at more reasonable prices.

Remember that although you may discover that sherried malts are very much to your liking, true distillery character is really only revealed when spirit is matured in a first-fill or refill cask. Sometimes it is hard to believe that the whisky you are drinking when comparing samples drawn from these differing maturation regimes has been distilled in the same place. One such example is the short-lived Pittyvaich Distillery (1975–1993) which was a blending whisky created by Arthur Bell & Sons. After the firm became part of United Distillers, a rich, sherried 12-year-old (43% abv) was released as part of the 'Flora and Fauna' series. The 2009 release of a 20-year-old (57.5% abv) matured in refill American oak casks reveals the real character of the spirit (see page 76).

The other point to take on board is the issue of the relevance of regional styles. Historically only two producing 'regions' used to exist, the Highlands and the Lowlands, separated by an imaginary line drawn up in the 1780s from Dumbarton to Dundee, either side of which was subject to differing excise regulations. In the Highlands the small-batch, pot-still process was employed whereas the Lowland distillers used the high-volume, large-batch, flash-distillation technique. With the rise of blending in the mid-to-late 19th century, malt distilleries were ranked by blenders into classes from Top, through First, Second and Third Class and generally speaking all the top-ranked whiskies were Speysides. Thus regional styles were applied and have tended to stick largely because the big distillers needed to manage large amounts of stock for blending in a comprehensible manner.

Nowadays the smaller distillers must innovate to survive and they are the exception that proves the rule. Many newcomers to the single malts might understandably expect all Islay malts to be peated. Not so … try Bruichladdich or Bunnahabhain and you will see what we mean. Jura is next door to Islay so it will be peated as well? No, it's a Highland malt in character. Speysides are fairly full, rich and sweet with no trace of peat? Try Ardmore and some of BenRiach's limited-release bottlings.

You may also find bottlings of Scotch in supermarkets that have names you do not recognise and many of these are created by the distillers for the retailers to sell as their own brands. Some are bottled along regional lines as Highland, Speyside or Islay malts and may be single or blended malts. They are often worth a try if only to introduce you to those regional styles we have just mentioned. Throughout the book we have also tried to point you in the direction of other whiskies to try as you proceed. These may be regionally close by, stylistically in the same mould … or maybe neither!

Since publication of the last *Malt Whisky Almanac* the actual definition of what is Scotch whisky has changed and we will deal with that in the next chapter. This area has been something of a hot potato over the last few years. For beginners what is important is to understand the difference between malt, blended and grain whisky as all of these are forms of Scotch whisky. Again, we'll come back to this shortly.

This book is a primer for those new to the world of Scotch whisky, a catch-up pocket guide for those who need a quick revision course and a handy aide-memoire for those lucky enough to work in the world of whisky and who need the salient facts and information readily to hand. Above all, it is the perfect companion if you are planning to visit any of the distilleries featured here — just remember to phone ahead or consult the distillery website to check on visiting times and tour details.

Enjoy your journey into the world of Scotch with *Whisky in Your Pocket*.

Wallace Milroy & Neil Wilson
London & Glasgow, September 2010.

1. What is Scotch Whisky?

WHEN you buy Scotch whisky it will come in a bottle. You can buy it in bulk in a cask, but very few people have the means to do this. There are **five** types of Scotch whisky which were redefined in November 2009. Exactly 100 years before a Royal Commission had defined what Scotch whisky was after a scandal involving the adulteration of whisky being sold in pubs. At that time whisky was distilled in two ways: in batches using pot stills and in a continuous method using the large, industrial patent still. Prior to the 1909 ruling, the Highland pot-still malt whisky distillers considered their whisky to be the true Scotch while the larger patent-still grain distillers were accused of passing off their less reputable whisky as the real thing. The commission settled the matter by stating that Scotch whisky was spirit distilled in Scotland from a mash of cereals which had been converted into soluble sugars by the action of the enzyme diastase contained within the malted portion of the mash. Effectively that meant that the produce of both distillation techniques was Scotch whisky.[1]

The finding was a victory for the Lowland patent-still producers and from that point onwards the industry evolved into what it is today: a worldwide, multi-million dollar success story. Put more simply, the type of Scotch whisky we drink today has just celebrated its centenary.

BLENDED SCOTCH

VARIABLE PROPORTION OF GRAIN

AND MALT WHISKIES

The bottle you buy will therefore contain one or other of these two types of whisky or a mixture of them. Under the new definitions the most common of the five forms of bottled whisky is **blended Scotch**.

Our graphic shows a typical bottle of this type of Scotch. This one is made up of 40% malt whisky and 60% grain whisky but these proportions will vary

---

[1] After the 1909 ruling some changes were made in 1915 requiring whisky to be matured in casks for at least three years. The strength at which whisky can be distilled must be no more than 94.8% alcohol.

from producer to producer. One popular blended Scotch, Teacher's Highland Cream, has a 45% malt whisky proportion. More commonly, the malt proportion is likely to be around 25%. The portion of malt can consist of as many individual malt whiskies as the blender decides to use

while the grain portion can also consist of more than one grain whisky but as there are only six grain distilleries in Scotland blenders tend to choose from a much reduced palette. Anyone shopping in a supermarket will see perhaps a dozen blended Scotch whiskies for sale including Johnnie Walker, Teacher's, Bell's, Whyte & Mackay, High Commissioner and The Famous Grouse. None of these brands carry an age statement on the label, but many of them issue aged expressions which are more expensive. The **minimum legal strength** for all five types of bottled Scotch is **40% abv** (alcohol by volume) and any age statement on the label will refer to the **youngest** whisky in the bottling, irrespective of whether it is within the malt portion or the grain portion.

The next category our supermarket shopper is likely to find is **single malt Scotch**. This whisky is produced in batches using the pot-still distilling process employed at all of Scotland's 96 active malt distilleries. Malt whisky is made from 100% malted barley, unlike grain whisky which is made from a mixture of cereals. Brands include Glenfiddich, Laphroaig, Macallan, Dalmore, Talisker, Highland Park, Jura, Bladnoch, Springbank and Glen Deveron amongst many others.

The contents of the bottle you purchase will contain pure malt whisky from the distillery named on the label which may, or may not, carry an age statement. If it does then the age of the youngest malt within the bottle will be

the age stated on the label. This is sometimes a confusing issue for the consumer but it shows that in order to produce a consistent bottling distillers will mix aged vintages of malt produced at the same distillery. So a bottle of single malt may contain malts distilled at different times from the same distillery. Rarer malts from single casks will carry an age statement and sometimes the number of the cask or bottle and the year of distillation as our Brora label displays. These will also be bottled at a higher strength than usual as these whiskies are not diluted down to the minimum legal strength of 40% abv.

The remaining categories represent altogether rarer types of Scotch whisky. **Blended malt Scotch** is a blend of two or more single malt Scotch whiskies from different distilleries.[2] Brands that fall into this category include Big Peat, Monkey Shoulder, Johnnie Walker Green Label and Spice Tree.

Blended grain Scotch is a blend of two or more single grain Scotch whiskies from different distilleries employing the patent-still distillation process. The Snow Grouse is the only readily available brand with the rarer and more

expensive Hedonism available from specialist retailers. The Hedonism label does not yet state that it is a blended grain whisky because the new regulations do not fully come into force until 2011 when it will have to carry the more specific description.

---

[2] Previously this was referred to as **vatted** malt Scotch whisky.

SINGLE GRAIN

100% GRAIN WHISKY FROM ONE DISTILLERY

Single grain Scotch is whisky from one grain distillery only. Cameron Brig is the most prominent trade bottling but is only available in Fife, where it is made, and from specialist retailers. Bottlings from defunct grain distilleries are available from independent bottlers and are generally very rare and very expensive.

Now that we know what Scotch whisky is, we can look at how it is made.

2. How is Scotch Whisky Made?

WE know that Scotch whisky exists in two forms: **malt** and **grain**. Now we need to look at how both are produced. Up to the point of **distillation**, the processes are very similar in that a low-alcohol beer is produced, called wash. Malt whisky **wash** is made from only malted barley, whereas grain whisky wash consists of some malted barley, but is predominately wheat-based with maize.

In both cases the cereals used contain energy-rich starch which will be used to produce alcohol but first it must be converted into soluble sugars. For malt whisky, the barley is **malted** by steeping in water for a couple of days, after which it is allowed to **germinate** over four days. This can be done on traditional **floor maltings** which used to exist in all distilleries but which are now confined to a few including Laphroaig, Bowmore and Balvenie where a proportion of the total malt requirement is made this way. [3] The last commercial floor maltings at Blackford in Perthshire closed in 1989 as it was too inefficient a method of producing malted barley on a large scale.

MAKING MALT WHISKY

FLOOR MALTINGS

The modern-day equivalents to floor maltings include the industrial drum maltings which operate in a number of locations around Scotland such as Glen Ord, Burghead

---

[3] Only Springbank in Campbeltown produces its entire malt requirement on its floor maltings as well as that of its sister distillery, Glengyle.

and Port Ellen. Other ways to create malt are the Saladin Box process (as seen at Tamdhu Distillery), the Wanderhaufen system and Tower Maltings but these last two are more prevalent on the continent. The processes of all these types of maltings might differ, but the result is the same.

Once the starch content has been converted it must be dried to stop further germination and maximize the sugar content. Distilleries that operate floor maltings do this on site by drying the barley in **kilns** topped by distinctive pagoda roofs. Depending on the flavour profile of the whisky, peat is used in varying quantities to aid this process and impart 'peatiness' to the malt which is measured as the phenolic content in parts per million (ppm). Many malt distilleries use unpeated malt while others like Laphroaig, Ardmore and Kilchoman, use peated malt at varying phenolic levels. Commercial maltings produce malt to the precise specifications of each individual distillery in large, efficient kilns employing the latest heat-reclamation and drying techniques. Kilning usually takes a couple of days. The grain distillers also use a proportion of this malt in the cereal mash they use as the enzyme, diastase, which is contained within the malt is key in breaking down the starch content of the wheat and maize.

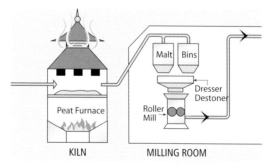

KILN   MILLING ROOM

Once the malt is ready it will be crisp, toasted and friable and is ready for **milling**. This is done by passing it through a dresser/destoner to remove undesirables before it is ground in a roller mill to a floury grist. In this state it is ready for **mashing**. In the **mash house**, it is piped into the **mashtun** with hot water and stirred to create a sweet, sugary liquor called **wort**. In the grain whisky process the ground wheat and maize portion of the mash is placed in a pressure cooker and made into a porridge which is then added to the mashtun. Once conversion is complete the mashtun is drained and the wort is processed via a vessel named the **underback** to the **wort cooler** and then transferred to the **fermentation** vessels in the **tun room**, known as **washbacks**, where **yeast** is added. The residue from the mashtun is processed into animal feed.

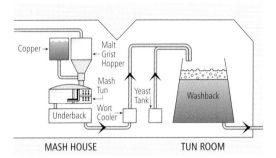

MASH HOUSE   TUN ROOM

Fermentation usually lasts a couple of days and creates a low-alcohol **beer** with a strength of 7–8% alcohol by volume (abv) and a lot of carbon dioxide which is lost to the atmosphere in most malt distilleries, but is of such significant volume in the grain whisky process that it is captured and processed. Once the wash is ready to be distilled the processes involved in creating malt and grain whisky diverge, so we will deal with malt whisky distillation first.

Malt whisky distilling

IN the **still house**, all malt whisky distilleries employ at least one pair of **pot** stills and sometimes an odd number of them. These are generally onion-shaped at the bottom with a rising, tapering neck section that then turns into a long pipe that carries the distillate away. The stills are generally heated with internal coils charged with steam; the rare exception being direct-fired stills with a gas burner beneath them. The principle of this technique is to distil the low-alcohol wash in the first still (the **wash still**) and to process that distillate (now around 21–23% abv) in the second still (the **low wines** or **spirit still**) to redistill it into spirit at around 67–68% abv. The distillate condenses by passing through the coil of copper pipe immersed in cold water in a **worm tub**, or more commonly, through a modern water-cooled **jacket condenser**.

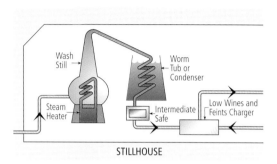

STILLHOUSE

Distillate from the wash still is captured in the **low wines and feints charger** before being used in the second distillation. The run of spirit from the spirit still is monitored and diverted back to the low wines and feints charger until the correct **strength** is obtained when it is diverted into the **spirit receiver**.

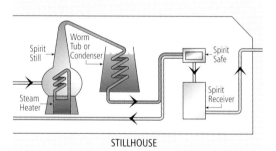

STILLHOUSE

The first part of the distillate that is discarded is called the **foreshots**, the important portion that is captured next is the **middle cut** and the last part, when the alcoholic volume starts to tail off, is called the **feints** which are again diverted to the low wines charger and redistilled in the next batch. The **stillman** makes the decision as to which part of the **spirit run** to collect by checking its strength as it flows through the **spirit safe**.[4] The middle cut is diverted into the spirit receiver tank before being piped to the **spirit store**.

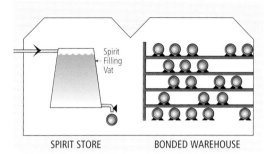

SPIRIT STORE   BONDED WAREHOUSE

The residue in the wash still is known as 'pot ale' and is processed into cattle food and usually mixed with the draff from the mashtun to form cattle cake. This process usually takes place at a 'dark grains' plant offsite, but some larger distilleries have their own facilities onsite to undertake this. The other by-product of the distillation process is the residue left in the spirit still which is known as the 'spent lees' and has to be discarded.

Some oddities have occurred in pot-still distilling practices, the Lomond Still probably being the most well known. These were pot stills with stubby, steam-heated column heads giving a thicker, heavier spirit and were first developed at Hiram Walker's Dumbarton complex in the 1950s. They have been used at Inverleven, Glenburgie (to create Glencraig malt), Miltonduff (Mosstowie) and Scapa where a variant of the still is the last one still in use in Scotland.

---

[4]Another 'intermediate safe' is employed to monitor the strength of the low wines before entering the low wines and feints charger from the wash still.

Grain whisky distilling

ALTHOUGH only carried out at six locations in Scotland, this process produces by far and away the largest proportion of Scotch whisky distilled each year in Scotland. The distilling process employed at these huge distilleries

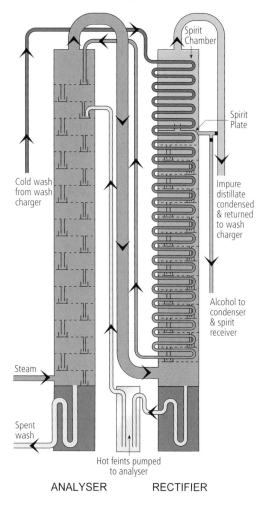

Spirit Chamber

Spirit Plate

Cold wash from wash charger

Impure distillate condensed & returned to wash charger

Steam

Alcohol to condenser & spirit receiver

Spent wash

Hot feints pumped to analyser

ANALYSER   RECTIFIER

is a **continuous** process which operates over a period of weeks and months, rather than hours and days. It was invented by Robert Stein of Kilbagie, Clackmannanshire in 1826 and then further developed and refined in 1831 by Aeneas Coffey, whose name is most closely related to the technique.

In its traditional form the still consists of two, tall, interlinked copper and stainless-steel columns, the **analyser** and the **rectifier**, which sit side-by-side. The basic principle is that pressure-fed steam enters the analyser at the base and rises up through a series of compartments separated by perforated sieve plates. As it does so, hot wash is fed in at the top of the analyser and descends through the compartments. The steam strips the alcohol from the wash and carries it over into the base of the rectifier, where it again ascends though another series of compartments. As it does so it comes into contact with the cold wash supply pipe which is routed through the rectifier in a series of loops and coils.[5] This acts as a surface on which the alcohol vapour condenses and the strength of the condensate increases as it rises up the rectifier until it is gathered on top of the unperforated **spirit plate** in the topmost compartment, the **spirit chamber**. The spirit this process produces is relatively flavourless compared to malt spirit, but is of a very high purity at around 94%.

Any uncondensed vapour is redistilled via the **wash charger** as is the fluid known as the **hot feints** which are piped away from the bottom of the rectifier and pumped back into the upper section of the analyser and redistilled.

Once the spirit has been collected the process returns to the same one as employed in the rest of Scotland's distilleries, the only differences being those of scale and location as some malt distilleries tanker their spirit offsite to facilities that are more suitable for cask-filling, maturing and warehousing.

In the **spirit store** the spirit is piped into the **spirit filling vat** where it is usually diluted down to the distiller's required strength (around 65% abv) before being measured into individual **casks**. A record of this procedure is

---

[5]Nowadays the wash is fed pre-heated into the analyser and a cold-water pipe acts as the condensing surface in the rectifier. Vacuum-distilling techniques are also more common in the modern-day patent still.

carefully logged for excise reports to the government. After this the spirit is subject to the producer's needs in terms of which wood it is matured in, how large the casks are, where it is held for maturing and for how long. The minimum term is **three years**, after which it can be used for bottling and blending. Almost all of the grain whisky produced in Scotland is released to be used in blending while the malts stocks are carefully monitored and managed to meet the requirements of the master blenders, many of whom have to source malts from other producers to create the blends in their own portfolios. This is when the value of **wood management** becomes apparent.

When spirit is first placed in a cask it is raw. From that point onwards the wood has an effect on it as the spirit interacts with the soluble constituents of the cask as it breathes, allowing the release of some alcoholic content which strengthens the remaining spirit volume.[6] Whisky is always matured in oak of either American or European extraction with most European oak being Spanish in origin. Casks that have previously held bourbon or sherry are common but there are no rules other than that the cask must be no more than 700 litres in volume and must be oak. Casks can be used more than once and can be rejuvenated by replacing old staves and also by de-charring and then re-charring the inside surface of the cask when the wood has become too tired.

Many producers and bottlers are now giving maturation details on the bottle labels and packaging so you might see that a malt whisky has been matured for 10 years in ex-bourbon and then finished for 18 months in Oloroso ex-sherry. Blended whiskies tend not to carry any maturation details.

---

[6] This loss is referred to as the 'Angels' Share' and amounts to 1–2% per annum of all maturing stocks in Scotland.

3. Single Malt Scotch Speyside

THE malts produced in this area of Scotland are perhaps the most obvious answer to the beginner's question, 'What does malt whisky taste like?' and it is more likely that anyone encountering malt for the first time will probably be trying a Glenfiddich or a Glenlivet. But that should not detract from the fact that malt whiskies are distilled over the length and breadth of Scotland and display a remarkable degree of variation.

This area contains the largest concentration of whisky-making apparatus in the world. In total there are 56 distilleries here of which 46 are active, four are mothballed, one is a living museum (Dallas Dhu), three others still exist but are defunct and unlikely ever to produce again (Coleburn, Convalmore and Parkmore) and one no longer exists (Pittyvaich). That makes 55. So where is the mystery distillery? It is Roseisle, the largest malt whisky distillery in the world which went into production in 2009 and has increased Diageo's capacity in the malt sector by 10%; a nod towards their forecast of greater stocks being required for the growing demand abroad in the emerging markets. For the purposes of this guide, I have not included three distilleries for the following reasons. Roseisle is less than three years old and is unlikely to become available in bottled form and the malt from William Grant & Sons' Kininvie Distillery in Dufftown is also not commercially available. The malt from defunct Parkmore does not exist in any form. There is, however, a new distillery in the planning stages at Huntly.

Speyside was also one of the most productive areas for illicit distilling in the 18th and early 19th centuries and gained a high reputation for the spirit it produced. In 1823 the government finally grasped the nettle and introduced legislation that encouraged illicit distillers to take out licences and it was George Smith of Glenlivet who was granted the first of these. He later moved the distillery to its current location at Minmore in 1858 where he conducted

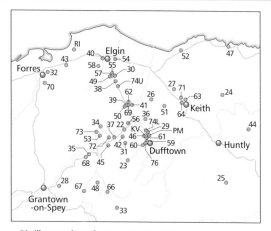

Distillery number refers to page number. U = upper, L = lower.
RI = Roseisle, KV = Kininvie, PM = Parkmore

business with his son, John. Stylistically the malts from this area are medium- to full-bodied, with some sweetness and they mature well around 10 to 15 years. Some producers age them even more but the bulk of them will be found in this age range. Many are matured in ex-sherry casks and this gives them a rich, savoury finish which is a hallmark of Speyside.

This area is one of the most beautiful in Scotland and there are good facilities at many of the distilleries for visitors. There is an established Speyside Malt Whisky Trail which consists of Benromach, Cardhu, Glenfiddich, Glen Grant, Glenlivet, Glen Moray, Strathisla and Dallas Dhu (which is the distillery museum I mentioned previously and is run by Historic Scotland) along with the Speyside Cooperage in Dufftown. Speyside also hosts two whisky festivals, one in the spring and one in autumn — both ideal times to be in the area (www.spiritofspeyside.com).

From a blending point of view, the Speysides form the backbone of most of the Scotch whisky blends that you will find. So why are they so important to the blender? Our friend Richard Paterson, master blender at Whyte & Mackay, draws an interesting comparison between the father of blending, Andrew Usher (1826–1898) and

Paul Cézanne, the father of modern art. The analogy is a good one in that the master blender 'draws from a palette of malt and grain whiskies to create his masterpieces. Harmony is his ultimate aim. No one colour, no one malt, must predominate.' This palette consists of a large number of malt whiskies and a relatively small number of grain whiskies. The Speysides form the largest part of the malt palette as the heavier and more smoky Islays are used sparingly due to their high degree of influence on a finished blend. Other robust malts from the Highlands, Islands and Campbeltown make distinct contributions to the blender's craft depending on their individual character. The floral, aromatic Lowlands help to create balance between these malts and integrate them with the larger grain whisky proportion.

In a word, Speyside is the heart of malt whisky distilling in Scotland and the malts we are now going to look at are the core bottlings which represent distillery character best. Most distilleries issue many more expressions and these can be discovered via the relevant Internet websites for each producer. Whiskies from lost distilleries such as Coleburn and Pittyvaich are available occasionally from their former proprietors, such as Diageo's Rare Malts selection and the discontinued Flora and Fauna series, or from the numerous specialist retailers and independent bottlers.

Malt	ABERLOUR
Pronounced	*Aber-LOWERR*
Distillery	Aberlour
	ABERLOUR
	AB38 9PJ
Owner	Pernod Ricard
Reception centre	01340 881249
Website	www.aberlour.com
Established	1826
Status	In production
Water source	Birkenbush and other springs
Malt source	Commercial maltsters
Phenolic content	Unpeated
Casks	Ex-bourbon and sherry
Annual output	3.7 million litres of alcohol
Stills	Wash: 2
	Spirit: 2
Main bottling	10 years old, 40%
Nose	Dry, fresh, fruity aromas of early autumn apples and pears enhanced with vanilla and mint toffee.
Taste	Smooth, creamy, spicy-sweet nutmeg and honey with the dewy freshness of autumn fruits.
Finish	Long, soft, warming.
Comments	A well-established, award-winning malt from Speyside.
Also try	Benrinnes, Benromach, Glenturret
Availability	Everywhere
Price	£25

Malt	**ALLT-A-BHAINNE**
Pronounced	*Olt-a-VAN-ya*
Distillery	Allt-a-Bhainne
	DUFFTOWN
	AB55 4DE
Owner	Pernod Ricard
Reception centre	No visitors
Established	1975
Status	In production
Water source	Springs on Benrinnes
Malt source	Commercial maltsters
Phenolic content	Unpeated and medium-peated
Casks	Refill hogsheads
Annual output	4 million litres of alcohol
Stills	Wash: 2
	Spirit: 2
Main bottling	Independents
Nose	Light, floral with herby notes.
Taste	Sweet and zesty, slightly spicy.
Finish	Refreshing.
Comments	A fine aperitif malt.
Also try	Glenburgie, Loch Lomond, Bladnoch
Availability	Specialist retailers
Price	£34 plus

Malt	AN CNOC
Pronounced	*a-NOCK*
Distillery	Knockdhu
	by HUNTLY
	AB54 7LJ
Owner	Thai Beverages
Reception centre	By appointment
Website	www.ancnoc.com
Established	1893-4
Status	In production
Water source	Four springs on the Knock Hill
Malt source	Local commercial maltsters
Phenolic content	Unpeated
Casks	Ex-bourbon and ex-sherry casks
Annual output	1.59 million litres of alcohol
Stills	Wash: 1
	Spirit: 1
Main bottling	12 years old, 40%
Nose	Soft, very aromatic with a hint of honey and lemon in the foreground.
Taste	Sweet to start with an appetising fruitiness.
Finish	Long and smooth. A malt for every occasion.
Comments	One of the five malts from the Inver House stable.
Also try	Knockando, Arran, Tamdhu
Availability	Specialist retailers
Price	£20 plus

Malt	ARDMORE
Pronounced	*Aard-MORE*
Distillery	Ardmore
	KENNETHMONT
	AB54 4NH
Owner	Fortune Brands
Website	www.ardmorewhisky.com
Established	1899
Status	In production
Water source	15 springs on Knockandy Hill
Malt source	Commercial maltsters
Phenolic content	12–14 ppm
Casks	Ex-bourbon and first-fill quarter casks.
Annual output	5 million litres of alcohol
Stills	Wash: 4
	Spirit: 4
Main bottling	No age statement, 46%
Nose	Creamy, rich, soft, smooth, slightly dry aroma with a hint of earthy peat.
Taste	Creamy peat tang with a touch of vanilla. After water, sweet ripe fruit with a tang of peat. Full-bodied.
Finish	Full, peppery, succulent, smooth and long.
Comments	A rare beast on Speyside ... a peated malt.
Also try	Glen Scotia, Bowmore, Fettercairn
Availability	Everywhere
Price	£25

Malt	**AUCHROISK**
Pronounced	*Oth-RUSK*
Distillery	Auchroisk
	MULBEN
	AB55 6XS
Owner	Diageo
Reception centre	By appointment
Website	www.malts.com
Established	1974
Status	In production
Water source	Dorie's Well
Malt source	Burghead Maltings
Phenolic content	Unpeated
Casks	Mostly ex-sherry
Annual output	3.6 million litres of alcohol
Stills	Wash: 4
	Spirit: 4
Main bottling	Rare Malts, Flora and Fauna and independent bottlings
Nose	Toffee and malt. Sweet pastry and a light fruitiness like tarte tatin.
Taste	Sweet malt with some acidity. Shortbread and spice. Trace of warm wood in development.
Finish	Warming and long.
Comments	One of Diageo's rare distillery bottlings.
Also try	Glen Keith, Glenrothes, Tormore
Availability	Specialist retailers
Price	£30 plus

Malt	AULTMORE
Pronounced	*Ollt-MORE*
Distillery	Aultmore
	KEITH
	AB55 6QY
Owner	Bacardi
Established	1897
Status	In production
Water source	Auchinderran Dam
Malt source	Commercial maltsters
Phenolic content	Unpeated
Casks	Ex-bourbon
Annual output	3.03 million litres of alcohol
Stills	Wash: 2
	Spirit: 2
Main bottling	12 years old, 40%
Nose	Floral perfume up front mingling with green apples.
Taste	Floral notes again merging with a richer, sweet and fruity character, reminiscent of a ripe plum pudding. Medium- to firm-bodied.
Finish	Satisfying, delicate and dry.
Comments	One of Bacardi's unsung malts.
Also try	Cardhu, Glengoyne, Arran
Availability	Specialist retailers
Price	£28–32

Malt	**BALMENACH**
Pronounced	*Baal-MENN-ach*
Distillery	Balmenach
	GRANTOWN-ON-SPEY
	PH26 3PF
Owner	Thai Beverages
Reception centre	By appointment
Website	www.inverhouse.com
Established	c.1824
Status	In production
Water source	Cromdale Burn
Malt source	Commercial maltsters
Phenolic content	Unpeated
Casks	Refill American and Spanish oak
Annual output	2 million litres of alcohol
Stills	Wash: 3
	Spirit: 3
Main bottling	Independents
Nose	Sherried, slightly smoky.
Taste	Full-bodied, vanilla overtones, sherry and spice notes.
Finish	Spicy, sherried and long-lasting.
Comments	The only malt in the Inver House stable which is not marketed as a brand.
Also try	Mortlach, Macallan, Dalmore
Availability	Specialist retailers
Price	£25 plus

Malt	BALVENIE
Pronounced	*Baal-VENN-ee*
Distillery	Balvenie
	DUFFTOWN
	AB55 4BB
Owner	William Grant & Sons Ltd
Reception centre	By appointment
Website	www.thebalvenie.com
Established	1892
Status	In production
Water source	Robbie Dubh Springs
Malt source	Floor maltings 10% local barley and commercial maltsters
Phenolic content	Unpeated
Casks	Ex-bourbon and sherry with some port pipes.
Annual output	6.5 million litres of alcohol
Stills	Wash: 5
	Spirit: 5
Main bottling	12 years old, 43%
Nose	Sweet fruit and Oloroso sherry notes, layered with honey and vanilla.
Taste	Smooth and mellow, nutty sweetness, cinnamon spiciness and a delicately proportioned layer of sherry.
Finish	Long and warming.
Comments	Glenfiddich's sister distillery.
Also try	BenRiach, Glendullan, Glenlivet
Availability	Everywhere
Price	£30

Malt	**BENRIACH**
Pronounced	*Ben-REE-ach*
Distillery	BenRiach
	ELGIN
	IV30 8SG
Owner	BenRiach Distillery Co Ltd
Website	www.benriachdistillery.co.uk
Established	1898
Status	In production
Water source	Burnside springs
Malt source	Commercial maltsters
Phenolic content	35 ppm and unpeated
Casks	Ex-bourbon, refill hogsheads and butts
Annual output	2.8 million litres of alcohol
Stills	Wash: 2
	Spirit: 2
Main bottling	No age statement, 40%
Nose	Honey, vanilla, floral, fruity with well balanced wood overtones.
Taste	Rounded medium- to full-bodied, rich honey, vanilla with hints of cream, spice and chocolate.
Finish	Delicate, dry refined aftertaste.
Comments	From an independent that is pushing the boundaries of what constitutes regional style.
Also try	Balvenie, Glen Ord, Royal Brackla
Availability	Widespread
Price	£20–25

Malt	BENRINNES
Pronounced	*Benn-RINN-iss*
Distillery	Benrinnes
	ABERLOUR
	AB38 9NN
Owner	Diageo
Website	www.malts.com
Established	c.1835
Status	In production
Water source	Rowantree and Scurran Burns
Malt source	Burghead and Roseisle Maltings
Phenolic content	Unpeated
Casks	Mainly European oak
Annual output	2.6 million litres of alcohol
Stills	Wash: 2
	Spirit: 4
Main bottling	Rare Malts, Special Releases and independent bottlings
Nose	Big and sweet. Muscular, caramelised fruits and sherry.
Taste	Full-bodied, big, powerful. Sweet, raisins, dates. After water, slightly smoky. Voluptuous.
Finish	Long, dry, warming, leaving traces of treacle and sandalwood.
Comments	Benrinnes employs its six stills in a form of triple distillation which is unique. Also available bottled as Stronachie.
Also try	Aberlour, Knockando, Stronachie
Availability	Specialist retailers
Price	£25 plus

Malt	BENROMACH
Pronounced	*Ben-ROMM-ach*
Distillery	Benromach
	FORRES
	IV36 3EB
Owner	Gordon & MacPhail Ltd
Reception centre	01309 675968
Website	www.benromach.com
Established	1898
Status	In production
Water source	Chapelton Springs in the Romach Hills
Malt source	Commercial maltsters
Phenolic content	Up to 10 ppm
Casks	Ex-bourbon and sherry and Oloroso
Annual output	750,000 litres of alcohol
Stills	Wash: 1
	Spirit: 1
Main bottling	10 years old, 43%
Nose	Charred oak influence and malt. Slightly nutty with pineapple and kiwi fruit.
Taste	Mouth-coating with toasted malt. Lingering sweet sherry and delicate peat smoke.
Finish	Long and lingering with subtle sherry and peat.
Comments	Rescued in 1993 by Gordon & MacPhail, this is a fine visitor attraction.
Also try	Edradour, Longmorn, Strathisla
Availability	Specialist retailers
Price	£35 plus

Malt	BRAES OF GLENLIVET
Distillery	Braeval BALLINDALLOCH AB37 9JS
Pronounced	*Bray-VAAL*
Owner	Pernod Ricard
Reception centre	N/a
Established	1973
Status	In production
Water source	Preenie and Katie Wells
Malt source	Commercial maltsters
Phenolic content	Unpeated
Casks	Ex-bourbon
Annual output	4 million litres of alcohol
Stills	Wash: 2 Spirit: 4
Main bottling	Independents
Nose	Light, dry with honey and fruity notes.
Taste	Medium-bodied, quite sweet with fruity overtones.
Finish	Some spice and a hint of smoke.
Comments	A blending whisky that is not widely available.
Also try	Benromach, Edradour, Cragganmore
Availability	Rare. Specialist retailers
Price	£55 plus

Malt	CARDHU
Pronounced	*Kaar-doo*
Distillery	Cardhu
	ABERLOUR
	AB38 7RZ
Owner	Diageo
Reception centre	01340 872555
Website	www.malts.com
Established	1824
Status	In production
Water source	Springs on Mannoch Hill and the Lyne Burn
Malt source	Burghead Maltings
Phenolic content	Unpeated
Casks	Refill ex-bourbon hogsheads
Annual output	3 million litres of alcohol
Stills	Wash: 3
	Spirit: 3
Main bottling	12 years old, 40%
Nose	Heady, pear drops, heather, resin and sweet honey-nut notes.
Taste	Medium-bodied. Well balanced, smooth mouthfeel; sweet and fresh then drying.
Finish	Lingering sweet smoke. Attractive, drying aftertaste.
Comments	A signature malt in the Johnnie Walker blends.
Also try	Glen Grant, Speyside, Tobermory
Availability	Widespread
Price	£30 plus

Malt	CRAGGANMORE
Pronounced	*Crag-ann-MORE*
Distillery	Cragganmore
	BALLINDALLOCH
	AB37 9AB
Owner	Diageo
Reception centre	01479 874700
Website	www.malts.com
Established	1869
Status	In production
Water source	Craggan Burn
Malt source	Roseisle Maltings
Phenolic content	Lightly peated.
Casks	Ex-bourbon and sherry
Annual output	1.6 million litres of alcohol
Stills	Wash: 2
	Spirit: 2
Main bottling	12 years old, 40%
Nose	Sweet floral fragrances with riverside herbs, flowers with some honey and vanilla.
Taste	Strong malty taste. Hints of sweet wood smoke and sandalwood. Firm, rounded, light to medium.
Finish	A long, malt-driven finish with light smoke and hints of sweetness.
Comments	A malty and complex dram.
Also try	Aberlour, Glenfarclas, Strathisla
Availability	Widespread
Price	£25–30

Malt	**CRAIGELLACHIE**
Pronounced	*Craig-ELL-achay*
Distillery	Craigellachie
	ABERLOUR
	AB38 9TF
Owner	Bacardi
Established	1891
Status	In production
Water source	Bluehill Quarry
Malt source	Commercial maltsters
Phenolic content	Unpeated
Casks	Ex-bourbon and sherry
Annual output	3.98 million litres of alcohol
Stills	Wash: 2
	Spirit: 2
Main bottling	14 years old, 40%
Nose	Rich, warm aroma of freshly baked pudding with a wisp of smoke and a hint of rubber.
Taste	Rich, malty flavour emerges from a syrupy palate with a sprinkling of crushed hazelnuts. Medium-bodied.
Finish	Long, delicately dry finish with a suggestion of charred oak.
Comments	Another constituent malt for the Dewar's blends.
Also try	Ardmore, Glenmorangie, Tamnavulin.
Availability	Specialist retailers
Price	£28–32

Malt	DAILUAINE
Pronounced	*Daal-EWE-ann*
Distillery	Dailuaine
	CARRON
	AB38 7RE
Owner	Diageo
Website	www.malts.com
Established	1851
Status	In production
Water source	Bailliemullich Burn
Malt source	Burghead Maltings
Phenolic content	Unpeated
Casks	Refill ex-bourbon hogsheads with some ex-sherry butts
Annual output	3.2 million litres of alcohol
Stills	Wash: 3
	Spirit: 3
Main bottling	16 years old, 43%
Nose	Full, rich, fruity aroma with honeysuckle overtones.
Taste	Full of Speyside flavour. Fruity, full-bodied, nutty, sweet.
Finish	Rich and dry with a long sweet aftertaste.
Comments	A great after-dinner dram.
Also try	Mortlach, Dalmore, GlenDronach
Availability	Specialist retailers
Price	£25 plus

Malt	**GLEN ELGIN**
Pronounced	*Glen ELL-gin*
Distillery	Glen Elgin
	ELGIN
	IV30 8SL
Owner	Diageo
Website	www.malts.com
Established	1900
Status	In production
Water source	Local springs near Milbuies Loch
Malt source	Burghead Maltings
Phenolic content	Unpeated
Casks	Ex-bourbon and sherry refills
Annual output	1.9 million litres of alcohol
Stills	Wash: 3
	Spirit: 3
Main bottling	12 years old, 43%
Nose	Battenburg cake and orange juice. Estery with water, fresh pears and a whiff of smoke.
Taste	Smooth, medium-bodied. Pleasant mouthfeel, sweetish, then dry with some acidity.
Finish	Slightly dry, well-balanced.
Comments	A top blending malt.
Also try	BenRiach, Glenlivet, Linkwood
Availability	Specialist retailers
Price	£25 plus

Malt	GLEN GRANT
Distillery	Glen Grant
	ROTHES
	AB38 7BS
Owner	Campari
Reception centre	01340 832118
Website	www.glengrant.com
Established	1840
Status	In production
Water source	Caperdonich Well
Malt source	Commercial maltsters
Phenolic content	Unpeated
Casks	Refill American oak casks
Annual output	5.9 million litres of alcohol
Stills	Wash: 4
	Spirit: 4
Main bottling	No age statement, 40%
Nose	Soft and slightly dry with a delicate fruity/ apple note.
Taste	Creamy and fruity.
Finish	Slightly nutty.
Comments	One of Italy's most popular malts.
Also try	An Cnoc, Glenallachie, Loch Lomond
Availability	Widespread
Price	£20 plus

Malt	**GLEN MORAY**
Distillery	Glen Moray
	ELGIN
	IV30 1YE
Owner	La Martiniquaise
Reception centre	01343 542577
Website	www.glenmoray.com
Established	1897
Status	In production
Water source	River Lossie
Malt source	Commercial maltsters
Phenolic content	Unpeated
Casks	First and refill ex-bourbon with some ex-sherry casks
Annual output	2 million litres of alcohol
Stills	Wash: 2
	Spirit: 2
Main bottling	No age statement, 40%
Nose	Fragrant, lightly drying, warming malty notes. Butterscotch, shortbread, fresh herbal/grassy notes.
Taste	Lightly spiced with a warming mouthfeel. Malty toffee sweetness, blackcurrants, fragrant citrus lemongrass tang.
Finish	Shortbread, fresh lemongrass, spicy ginger marmalade.
Comments	Excellent distillery to visit. Now under foreign ownership once more.
Also try	Bladnoch, Glenallachie, Deanston
Availability	Everywhere
Price	£20 plus

Malt	**GLEN SPEY**
Distillery	Glen Spey
	ROTHES
	AB38 7AT
Owner	Diageo
Website	www.malts.com
Established	1878
Status	In production
Water source	Doonie Burn
Malt source	Burghead Maltings
Phenolic content	Unpeated
Casks	Refill ex-bourbon hogsheads
Annual output	1.5 million litres of alcohol
Stills	Wash: 2
	Spirit: 2
Main bottling	Managers' Choice and independent bottlings
Nose	Strikingly aromatic and fragrant.
Taste	Very full palate, strong overtones of ripe fruit and a light smokiness.
Finish	Nuances of smoke which finishes smoothly.
Comments	An after-dinner dram. Much of the production goes into the J&B blend.
Also try	Glen Keith, Glenfiddich, Speyburn
Availability	Specialist retailers
Price	£30 plus

Malt	**GLENALLACHIE**
Pronounced	*Glen-ALLA-chay*
Distillery	Glenallachie
	ABERLOUR
	AB38 9LR
Owner	Pernod Ricard
Established	1967–8
Status	In production
Water source	Henshead and Blackstank Burns
Malt source	Commercial maltsters
Phenolic content	Unpeated
Casks	Refill hogsheads, butts and barrels
Annual output	3 million litres of alcohol
Stills	Wash: 2
	Spirit: 2
Main bottling	Independents
Nose	Elegant with a delightful floral bouquet.
Taste	Well balanced. Smooth with a hint of honey and fruit.
Finish	Light and sweet.
Comments	One of the three distilleries created by Welshman William Delmé-Evans.
Also try	Balvenie, Caperdonich, Tomintoul
Availability	Specialist retailers
Price	£24 plus

Malt	GLENBURGIE
Pronounced	*Glen-BURR-gay*
Distillery	Glenburgie
	FORRES
	IV36 2QY
Owner	Thai Beverages
Reception centre	By appointment
Established	1810
Status	In production
Water source	Local springs and borehole aquifer
Malt source	Commercial maltsters
Phenolic content	Unpeated
Casks	Refill hogsheads, butts and barrels
Annual output	4.2 million litres of alcohol
Stills	Wash: 3
	Spirit: 3
Main bottling	Independents
Nose	Fragrant, floral aroma with hints of fruit.
Taste	Light, delicate, aromatic flavour of honey and maple.
Finish	Pleasant but quite short.
Comments	A refreshing malt for pre-dinner drinking. Distillery is beautifully situated.
Also try	Glen Grant, Caperdonich, Inchgower
Availability	Specialist retailers
Price	£25 plus

Malt	**GLENDRONACH**
Pronounced	*Glen-DRONN-ach*
Distillery	GlenDronach
	FORGUE
	AB54 6DB
Owner	BenRiach Distillery Co Ltd
Reception centre	01466 730202
Website	www.glendronachdistillery.co.uk
Established	1826
Status	In production
Water source	Private springs
Malt source	Commercial maltsters
Phenolic content	Lightly peated
Casks	Ex-bourbon and sherry
Annual output	1.4 million litres of alcohol
Stills	Wash: 2
	Spirit: 2
Main bottling	15 years old, 40%
Nose	Incredible concentration of aromas. Treacle toffee and chocolate orange.
Taste	A very dynamic and full-bodied dram for its age. Chewy with coffee, chocolate and treacle scones.
Finish	Long-lasting with smoky overtones. Memorable.
Comments	A big whisky for after-dinner drinking.
Also try	Dalmore, Macallan, Mortlach
Availability	Widespread
Price	£30 plus

Malt	**GLENFARCLAS**
Pronounced	*Glen-FAAR-class*
Distillery	Glenfarclas
	BALLINDALLOCH
	AB37 9BD
Owner	J & G Grant
Reception centre	01807 500345
Website	www.glenfarclas.com
Established	1836
Status	In production
Water source	The Green Burn on Ben Rinnes
Malt source	Commercial maltsters
Phenolic content	1–3 ppm
Casks	Ex-sherry and plain oak
Annual output	Confidential
Stills	Wash: 3
	Spirit: 3
Main bottling	10 years old, 40%
Nose	Sherry-sweet malty tones with delicate smokiness, releasing subtle spices. Warming the glass reveals honey, vanilla and pear drops.
Taste	Light, with a mouth-watering combination of malt, smoke and sherry sweetness. Hints of dried fruit, vanilla, cinnamon and cloves.
Finish	Long, smooth and spicy, with a delicious, yet delicate, lingering smokiness.
Comments	A big, classic Speyside malt for after dinner.
Also try	Glenlivet, Dalmore, Mortlach
Availability	Widespread
Price	£28–30

Malt	GLENFIDDICH
Pronounced	*Glen-FIDD-ich*
Distillery	Glenfiddich
	DUFFTOWN
	AB55 4DH
Owner	William Grant & Sons Ltd
Reception centre	01340 820373
Website	www.glenfiddich.com
Established	1886–7
Status	In production
Water source	Robbie Dubh Springs
Malt source	Commercial maltsters
Phenolic content	Unpeated
Casks	American and European oak
Annual output	11 million litres of alcohol
Stills	Wash: 10
	Spirit: 18
Main bottling	12 years old, 40%
Nose	Fresh and fruity with a hint of pear. Beautifully crafted single malt with a delicately balanced fragrance.
Taste	Characteristic sweet, fruity notes. Develops into elements of butterscotch, cream, malt and subtle oak flavour.
Finish	Long, smooth and mellow.
Comments	The world's most popular single malt.
Also try	Aberlour, Glenallachie, Glenglassaugh
Availability	Everywhere
Price	£25 plus

Malt	**GLENGLASSAUGH**
Pronounced	*Glen-GLASS-och*
Distillery	Glenglassaugh
	PORTSOY
	AB45 2SQ
Owner	Scaent Group
Reception centre	By appointment
Website	www.glenglassaugh.com
Established	1875
Status	In production
Water source	Wells near the Glassaugh Spring
Malt source	Commercial maltsters
Phenolic content	Unpeated
Casks	Ex-bourbon, refill hogsheads and ex-sherry butts
Annual output	1.1 million litres of alcohol
Stills	Wash: 1
	Spirit: 1
Main bottling	26 years old, 46%
Nose	Rich sherry aromas, eucalyptus and cedar followed by a medley of boiled fruits.
Taste	Rich, dried fruit dominates with the boiled fruits in mid-palate. Hints of vanilla, spices and salt.
Finish	Long, rich and fruity.
Comments	A welcome return for a fine malt. Bottled on site.
Also try	Banff, Glen Deveron, Inchgower
Availability	Distillery and specialist retailers
Price	£150

Malt	**GLENLIVET**
Distillery	Glenlivet
	BALLINDALLOCH
	AB37 9DB
Owner	Pernod Ricard
Reception centre	01340 821720
Website	www.theglenlivet.com
Established	1824
Status	In production
Water source	Josie's and Blairfindy's Wells
Malt source	Crisps of Port Gordon
Phenolic content	Unpeated
Casks	Ex-bourbon and sherry
Annual output	10.5 million litres of alcohol
Stills	Wash: 7
	Spirit: 7
Main bottling	12 years old, 40%
Nose	Perfectly balanced fruity aroma with delicate floral fragrance and vanilla/honey sweetness.
Taste	Soft, smooth balance of sweet summer fruits and the floral fragrance of spring flowers.
Finish	Lingering and gentle.
Comments	The classic Speyside? Just expanded and now one of Scotland's largest malt distilleries.
Also try	Glenfarclas, Mortlach, Glenfiddich
Availability	Everywhere
Price	£30

Malt	**GLENLOSSIE**
Pronounced	*Glen-LOSS-ay*
Distillery	Glenlossie
	ELGIN
	IV30 8SS
Owner	Diageo
Website	N/a
Established	1876
Status	In production
Water source	Bardon Burn
Malt source	Burghead Maltings
Phenolic content	Unpeated
Casks	Ex-bourbon casks
Annual output	2.3 million litres of alcohol
Stills	Wash: 3
	Spirit: 3
Main bottling	Flora and Fauna and independent bottlings
Nose	Fresh, light with plenty of aromatic citrus notes.
Taste	Zesty and refreshing. Light-bodied with lemon and citrus overtones.
Finish	Effervescent and refreshing.
Comments	A great aperitif whisky.
Also try	Glen Grant, Knockando, Glen Moray
Availability	Specialist retailers
Price	£35 plus

Malt	**GLENROTHES**
Pronounced	*Glen-ROTH-ess*
Distillery	Glenrothes
	ROTHES
	AB38 7AA
Owner	Berry Brothers & Rudd
Website	www.glenrotheswhisky.com
Established	1878
Status	In production
Water source	Ardcanny and Brauchhill Spring
Malt source	Simpson's, Berwick-Upon-Tweed malted at Tamdhu Distillery Maltings
Phenolic content	Unpeated
Casks	Refill ex-sherry Spanish and American oak and small proportion of ex-bourbon
Annual output	4.4 million litres of alcohol
Stills	Wash: 5
	Spirit: 5
Main bottling	12 years old, 43%
Nose	American oak vanilla and coconut, hint of plums.
Taste	Full malty flavour, medium-sweet, vanilla and orange zest.
Finish	Long and slightly spicy.
Comments	A first-class malt. The brand is now owned by Berry Brothers & Rudd although the distillery remains in Edrington ownership.
Also try	Aberlour, Fettercairn, Miltonduff
Availability	Specialist retailers
Price	£32 plus

Malt	GLENTAUCHERS
Pronounced	*Glenn-TOCH-ers*
Distillery	Glentauchers
	KEITH
	AB55 6YL
Owner	Pernod Ricard
Established	1898
Status	In production
Water source	Rosarie Burn
Malt source	Commercial maltsters
Phenolic content	Unpeated
Casks	Ex-bourbon hogsheads
Annual output	3.4 million litres of alcohol
Stills	Wash: 3
	Spirit: 3
Main bottling	Independents
Nose	Fresh and sweet, rounded with hints of butter toffees.
Taste	Sweet with delicate hints of malty cereal notes. Mouth warming and fresh.
Finish	Long and fresh.
Comments	A key malt in the Ballantine's blend.
Also try	Aultmore, Glengoyne, Tamdhu
Availability	Specialist retailers
Price	£30 plus

Malt	INCHGOWER
Pronounced	*Inch-GOW-err*
Distillery	Inchgower
	BUCKIE
	AB56 5AB
Owner	Diageo
Website	www.malts.com
Established	1871
Status	In production
Water source	Springs in the Menduff Hills
Malt source	Burghead Maltings
Phenolic content	Unpeated
Casks	Refill American oak casks
Annual output	1.9 million litres of alcohol
Stills	Wash: 2
	Spirit: 2
Main bottling	Special Releases, Flora and Fauna and independent bottlings
Nose	Vanilla, then dune-grass and sea air with a hint of eucalyptus.
Taste	Sweetish and almost minty (the eucalyptus?) with some acidity; sweet and sour?
Finish	Dries gently to a medium-length finish that's fresh and very slightly bitter.
Comments	Interesting post-dinner dram.
Also try	Glenglassaugh, Glentauchers, Tullibardine
Availability	Rare. Specialist retailers
Price	£30 plus

Malt	KNOCKANDO
Pronounced	*Nock-AAN-du*
Distillery	Knockando
	KNOCKANDO
	AB38 7RT
Owner	Diageo
Website	www.malts.com
Established	1898
Status	In production
Water source	Cardnach Spring
Malt source	Burghead Maltings
Phenolic content	Lightly peated
Casks	Refill ex-bourbon hogsheads
Annual output	1.5 million litres of alcohol
Stills	Wash: 2
	Spirit: 2
Main bottling	12 years old, 40%
Nose	Fruity-floral, hint of blackcurrant. Water brings up cereal notes and meaty aromas.
Taste	Light-bodied with light mouthfeel, central on the palate. Drying lightly with a trace of acidity.
Finish	Relatively short. Clean and easy to drink.
Comments	A big constituent in J&B blends.
Also try	Aberlour, Glenfarclas, Longmorn
Availability	Specialist retailers
Price	£20-25

Malt	LINKWOOD
Distillery	Linkwood
	ELGIN
	IV30 8RQ
Owner	Diageo
Website	www.malts.com
Established	1825
Status	In production
Water source	Springs near Milbuies Loch
Malt source	Burghead Maltings
Phenolic content	Unpeated
Casks	Refill American hogsheads and some refill European butts
Annual output	2.25 million litres of alcohol
Stills	Wash: 3
	Spirit: 3
Main bottling	Managers' Choice and independent bottlings
Nose	Deep and fruity, but creamy and rich. With water, cherries, plums and brown sugar emerge.
Taste	Light to medium-bodied, syrupy, smooth and fruity, sweet to taste.
Finish	Spicy, drying and long. Nutmeg, even traces of snuff.
Comments	Another malt distilled for Diageo's blends.
Also try	Glen Elgin, Glenlivet, Speyside
Availability	Specialist retailers
Price	£35 plus

Malt	LONGMORN
Distillery	Longmorn
	ELGIN
	IV30 8SJ
Owner	Pernod Ricard
Established	1894–5
Status	In production
Water source	Borehole aquifer
Malt source	Commercial maltsters
Phenolic content	Unpeated
Casks	Ex-bourbon and sherry refills
Annual output	3.5 million litres of alcohol
Stills	Wash: 4
	Spirit: 4
Main bottling	16 years old, 48%
Nose	Spicy, sweet and fruity. Touch of caramel.
Taste	Effervescent and spicy with exotic fruits and a herbal freshness.
Finish	Long and lingering with gingery spice. Highly complex.
Comments	Changes in distilling practices in the early 1990s might bring some changes to matured stocks. We shall see.
Also try	Aberlour, Glenfarclas, Strathisla
Availability	Specialist retailers
Price	£43

Malt	MACALLAN
Pronounced	*Mac-ALLAN*
Distillery	Macallan
	CRAIGELLACHIE
	AB38 9RX
Owner	Edrington Group
Reception centre	01340 871471
Website	www.themacallan.com
Established	1824
Status	In production
Water source	Borehole aquifers
Malt source	Simpson's, Berwick-Upon-Tweed
Phenolic content	Unpeated
Casks	First-fill and refill ex-sherry Spanish and American oak, some ex-bourbon
Annual output	8.6 million litres of alcohol
Stills	Wash: 7
	Spirit: 14
Main bottling	10 years old, 40%
Nose	A hint of sweet toffee balanced with dried fruit and sherry.
Taste	Smooth with dried fruits, sherry sweetness and wood smoke.
Finish	Dried fruits with sweet toffee and a hint of wood spice.
Comments	One of the great Speysides. Available in a wide range of finishes.
Also try	Balmenach, Mortlach, Dalmore
Availability	Everywhere
Price	£27 plus

Malt	MANNOCHMORE
Pronounced	*Man-och-MORE*
Distillery	Mannochmore
	ELGIN
	IV30 8SS
Owner	Diageo
Website	www.malts.com
Established	1971
Status	In production
Water source	Bardon Burn
Malt source	Burghead Maltings
Phenolic content	Lightly peated
Casks	Refill American hogsheads
Annual output	3.2 million litres of alcohol
Stills	Wash: 3
	Spirit: 3
Main bottling	Rare Malts, Special Releases and independent bottlings
Nose	Damp earth then autumn fruits, a hint of smoke and some orange citrus.
Taste	Light-bodied, tongue-coating. Cereal and citrus with tarte au chocalat, fruit compote. Boiled fruit sweets.
Finish	Long, hot, persistent, yet smooth, silky, warm and delicate. Fragrant rosewater aftertaste.
Comments	Glenlossie's sister distillery.
Also try	Auchentoshan, Glenlossie, Tomintoul
Availability	Specialist retailers
Price	£35 plus

Malt	MILTONDUFF
Pronounced	*Mil-ton-DUFF*
Distillery	Miltonduff
	ELGIN
	IV30 8TQ
Owner	Pernod Ricard
Established	1824
Status	In production
Water source	The Black Burn and borehole aquifer
Malt source	Kilgours of Kirkcaldy
Phenolic content	Unpeated
Casks	Ex-bourbon
Annual output	5.5 million litres of alcohol
Stills	Wash: 3
	Spirit: 3
Main bottling	Independents
Nose	Fruity, raisins with fragrant heather and cereal notes.
Taste	Light-bodied. Sweet, fruity cereal flavours with a spicy edge. Floral, freshly cut grass notes.
Finish	Balanced, sweet and well-rounded.
Comments	Until 1981 Mosstowie malt was also produced at Miltonduff in Lomond stills.
Also try	Tomatin, Teaninich, Glen Spey
Availability	Specialist retailers
Price	£25 plus

Malt	MORTLACH
Distillery	Mortlach
	DUFFTOWN
	AB55 4AQ
Owner	Diageo
Website	www.malts.com
Established	1823
Status	In production
Water source	Local springs
Malt source	Burghead Maltings
Phenolic content	Unpeated
Casks	Refill European casks
Annual output	2.9 million litres of alcohol
Stills	Wash: 3
	Spirit: 3
Main bottling	Managers' Choice and independent bottlings
Nose	Full, pleasant, well-rounded floral aroma with a touch of smoke. Refreshing.
Taste	Rich and full with a hint of smoke and a pronounced Speyside sweetness.
Finish	Long, smooth, full sherried finish.
Comments	First-class after-dinner malt.
Also try	GlenDronach, Dailuaine, Dalmore
Availability	Specialist retailers
Price	£35 plus

Malt	**THE SINGLETON OF DUFFTOWN**
Distillery	Dufftown DUFFTOWN AB55 4ER
Owner	Diageo
Website	www.malts.com
Established	1896
Status	In production
Water source	Jock's Well in the Conval Hills
Malt source	Burghead Maltings
Phenolic content	Unpeated
Casks	Ex-bourbon and sherry refills
Annual output	5.8 million litres of alcohol
Stills	Wash: 3 Spirit: 3
Main bottling	12 years old, 40%
Nose	Toasted hazelnut and rich fruit. Water brings out fruit-sweet aromas.
Taste	Sweetness, crunchy nuts, then smooth fruity richness. Hints of blackcurrant, brown sugar and espresso coffee.
Finish	Medium to long, elegantly drying and crisp with a delayed, lingering warmth.
Comments	A major component in Bell's Original blend.
Also try	Pittyvaich, Glen Spey, Speyburn
Availability	Everywhere
Price	£30

Malt	THE SINGLETON OF GLENDULLAN
Distillery	Glendullan DUFFTOWN AB55 4DJ
Owner	Diageo
Reception centre	By appointment
Website	www.malts.com
Established	1897–8
Status	In production
Water source	River Fiddich
Malt source	Burghead Maltings
Phenolic content	Unpeated
Casks	Ex-bourbon refill hogsheads and some European oak
Annual output	3.7 million litres of alcohol
Stills	Wash: 3 Spirit: 3
Main bottling	12 years old, 40%
Nose	Rich, deep and fruity with toasted, nutty notes.
Taste	Smooth, sweet then dry with figs, cooked pastry and tea notes.
Finish	A clean, fresh medium-length finish. Sustaining and substantial. Lingering warmth.
Comments	More likely to be found in export markets and at the distillery.
Also try	Glenfiddich, Balvenie, Glenlivet
Availability	Specialist retailers
Price	£30 plus

Malt	**SPEYBURN**
Distillery	Speyburn
	ABERLOUR
	AB38 7AG
Owner	Thai Beverages
Reception centre	By appointment
Website	www.inverhouse.com
Established	1897
Status	In production
Water source	Granty Burn sourced on the western slope of the Glen of Rothes
Malt source	Commercial maltsters
Phenolic content	Unpeated
Casks	Ex-bourbon casks
Annual output	1.8 million litres of alcohol
Stills	Wash: 1
	Spirit: 1
Main bottling	10 years old, 40%
Nose	Fresh, clean and aromatic with a rich lemony fruitiness.
Taste	Medium-bodied with a delicate, fruity character.
Finish	Dry, warm and peaty.
Comments	One of the five malts from the Inver House stable. A beautifully located distillery.
Also try	Pittyvaich, Glen Spey, Longmorn
Availability	Specialist retailers
Price	£20 plus

Malt	**STRATHISLA**
Pronounced	*Strath-EYE-la*
Distillery	Strathisla
	KEITH
	AB55 5BS
Owner	Pernod Ricard
Reception centre	01542 783044
Website	www.maltwhiskydistilleries.com
Established	1786
Status	In production
Water source	Broomhill and Newmill Spring
Malt source	Paul's Malt of Buckie
Phenolic content	Unpeated
Casks	Ex-bourbon and sherry refills
Annual output	2.4 million litres of alcohol
Stills	Wash: 2
	Spirit: 2
Main bottling	12 years old, 43%
Nose	Rich and fruity with a complex array of hay-like aromas balanced with a dry oakiness.
Taste	Full, fruity and hay-like flavours with a mellow nutty sweetness.
Finish	Rich and mellow.
Comments	A striking, romantic-looking distillery.
Also try	Aberfeldy, Cragganmore, Longmorn
Availability	Specialist retailers
Price	£25 plus

Malt	STRATHMILL
Pronounced	*Strath-MILL*
Distillery	Strathmill
	KEITH
	AB55 5DQ
Owner	Diageo
Website	www.malts.com
Established	1891
Status	In production
Water source	Local springs
Malt source	Burghead Maltings
Phenolic content	Unpeated
Casks	Refill hogsheads and ex-sherry butts
Annual output	2.3 million litres of alcohol
Stills	Wash: 2
	Spirit: 2
Main bottling	Managers' Choice and independent bottlings
Nose	Delicate, soft and fruity. Cut grass as well.
Taste	Very smooth with vanilla overtones and a hint of spice.
Finish	Grassy and herbal, slightly spicy.
Comments	This was an unobtainable malt a decade ago and is still difficult to find.
Also try	Pittyvaich, Oban, Tamnavulin
Availability	Rare. Specialist retailers
Price	£30 plus

Malt	STRONACHIE
Pronounced	*Stronn-ACHAY*
Distillery	Benrinnes
	ABERLOUR
	AB38 9NN
Owner	A D Rattray Ltd
Website	www.stronachie.com
Established	c.1835
Status	In production
Water source	Rowantree and Scurran Burns
Malt source	Burghead and Roseisle Maltings
Phenolic content	Unpeated
Casks	Mainly European oak
Annual output	2.6 million litres of alcohol
Stills	Wash: 2
	Spirit: 4
Main bottling	12 years old, 43%
Nose	Sour dough, spiced apples, raisins, pear drops.
Taste	Medium-to full-bodied, spicy, invigorating. Spiced fruit cake, raisins, cinnamon and cloves.
Finish	Sweet woody notes and prominent peat smoke evolve in the mouth to leave a drying aftertaste.
Comments	This unique malt is a close match to the 1904 bottling of Stronachie in Kinross-shire which closed in the 1920s.
Also try	Benrinnes, Cragganmore, Scapa
Availability	Specialist retailers
Price	£25–30

Malt	TAMNAVULIN
Pronounced	*Tamna-VOOL-inn*
Distillery	Tamnavulin
	BALLINDALLOCH
	AB37 9JA
Owner	United Spirits
Established	1966
Status	In production
Water source	Local springs
Malt source	Commercial maltsters
Phenolic content	Trace
Casks	First-fill ex-bourbon
Annual output	4.2 million litres of alcohol
Stills	Wash: 3
	Spirit: 3
Main bottling	12 years old, 40%
Nose	Light and fragrant with soft, floral, grapey notes and a hint of dewy grass in the background.
Taste	Dry and firm. Delicate fruity tones released onto the palate. Refined.
Finish	Refreshing, rather like having just finished a fine herbal tea.
Comments	A blending malt used in Whyte & Mackay.
Also try	Glenmorangie, Craigellachie, Teaninich
Availability	Specialist retailers
Price	£25 plus

Malt	TOMINTOUL
Pronounced	*Tom-in-TOWEL*
Distillery	Tomintoul
	BALLINDALLOCH
	AB37 9AQ
Owner	Angus Dundee Distillers plc
Website	www.tomintouldistillery.co.uk
Established	1964–5
Status	In production
Water source	Ballantruan Spring
Malt source	Commercial maltsters
Phenolic content	Unpeated
Casks	Refill and first-fill hogsheads and some Oloroso ex-sherry butts
Annual output	3.3 million litres of alcohol
Stills	Wash: 2
	Spirit: 2
Main bottling	12 years old, 40%
Nose	Round, creamy with subtle hints of sherry sweetness.
Taste	Soft, smooth and elegant with a delicate sherry presence.
Finish	Mellow and soothing.
Comments	Now owned by a small independent distiller, this malt should become more available.
Also try	Bladnoch, Glenkinchie, Glen Moray
Availability	Widespread
Price	£23 plus

Malt	TORMORE
Pronounced	*Torr-MORE*
Distillery	Tormore
	GRANTOWN-ON-SPEY
	PH26 3LR
Owner	Pernod Ricard
Established	1958–60
Status	In production
Water source	Achvochkie Burn
Malt source	Commercial maltsters
Phenolic content	Unpeated
Casks	Refill American ex-bourbon casks
Annual output	3.7 million litres of alcohol
Stills	Wash: 4
	Spirit: 4
Main bottling	12 years old, 40%
Nose	Gentle citrus notes and toasted almonds.
Taste	Smooth and soft, a gentle citrus tang balanced with subtle spices.
Finish	Rounded, long-lasting and complex.
Comments	Back on the UK market.
Also try	Deanston, Tomintoul, Glenfiddich
Availability	Widespread
Price	£23 plus

Malt	CAPERDONICH
Pronounced	*Kapper-DONN-ich*
Distillery	Caperdonich
	ROTHES
	AB38 7BS
Owner	Pernod Ricard
Established	1898. Closed 1902. Re-established 1965.
Status	Mothballed
Water source	Caperdonich Burn
Malt source	Commercial maltsters
Phenolic content	Unpeated
Casks	Offsite in refill casks
Annual output	2.1 million litres of alcohol
Stills	Wash: 2
	Spirit: 2
Main bottling	Independents
Nose	A light, very delicate fragrance of peat.
Taste	Medium, with a slight hint of fruit.
Finish	Fragrant, quick and smoky.
Comments	The owners have no plans to reinstate production of this malt at present.
Also try	Bunnahabhain, Glenburgie, Tomintoul
Availability	Rare. Specialist retailers
Price	£30 plus

Malt	DALLAS DHU
Pronounced	*Dallas Doo*
Distillery	Dallas Dhu
	FORRES
	IV36 2RR
Owner	Diageo
Reception centre	01309 676548
Website	www.malts.com
Established	1899. Closed 1983.
Status	Mothballed
Water source	Altyre Burn
Stills	Wash: 1
	Spirit: 1
Main bottling	Rare Malts and independent bottlings
Nose	Really rich and full, interwoven with oak smoke, sweetness and malt.
Taste	Rich, full, clinging and malty with every element in harmony.
Finish	Beautiful finish with haunting traces of oak.
Comments	The distillery is in the care of Historic Scotland as a living museum.
Also try	Dailuaine, GlenDronach, Macallan
Availability	Rare. Specialist retailers
Price	£60 plus

Malt	**GLEN KEITH**
Distillery	Glen Keith
	KEITH
	AB55 5BU
Owner	Pernod Ricard
Established	1957–8
Status	Mothballed
Water source	Balloch Hill Springs
Phenolic content	Unpeated
Stills	Wash: 3
	Spirit: 3
Main bottling	10 years old, 43%
Nose	Orchard fruits with a hint of vanilla.
Taste	Sweet and fruity with floral notes and some vanilla.
Finish	Zesty and spicy.
Comments	There are no plans to reinstate the distillery.
Also try	Deanston, Glenrothes, Tormore
Availability	Specialist retailers
Price	£30 plus

Malt	IMPERIAL
Distillery	Imperial
	ABERLOUR
	AB38 7QP
Owner	Pernod Ricard
Established	1897
Status	Mothballed
Water source	Ballintomb Burn
Stills	Wash: 2
	Spirit: 2
Main bottling	Independents
Nose	Sweet chocolate, malty. Spicy with dusted fruit notes. Rounded.
Taste	Aniseed and eucalyptus. Strong winey notes like a cognac. Some toasted malt. Light-bodied, well balanced.
Finish	Rich fruit with sweet malt.
Comments	Imperial is uniquely constructed of red brick and until 1955 had a crown-topped pagoda.
Also try	Inchgower, Glenglassaugh, Glenallachie
Availability	Specialist retailers
Price	£35 plus

Malt	**TAMDHU**
Pronounced	*Taam-DOO*
Distillery	Tamdhu
	ABERLOUR
	AB38 7RP
Owner	Edrington Group
Website	www.edringtongroup.com
Established	1896–7
Status	Mothballed
Water source	Borehole and springs beneath the distillery
Malt source	100% Saladin box maltings
Phenolic content	Unpeated
Casks	Refill ex-sherry Spanish and American oak, some ex-bourbon
Annual output	4 million litres of alcohol
Stills	Wash: 3
	Spirit: 3
Main bottling	No age statement, 40%
Nose	Light aroma with a trace of honey sweetness.
Taste	Medium-bodied with a little fruity sweetness.
Finish	Very mellow.
Comments	Not as available or popular as it once was.
Also try	Arran, Aultmore, Speyside
Availability	Specialist retailers
Price	£20–23

Malt	**COLEBURN**	
Pronounced	*COAL-burn*	
Distillery	Coleburn	
Website	www.malts.com	
Established	1897. Closed 1985.	
Status	Lost	
Main bottling	Rare Malts and independent bottlings	
Nose	Light, flowery, slightly oily.	
Taste	Light, clean, crisp with hints of spicy oak and citrus zest.	
Finish	Refreshing, slightly peppery.	
Comments	Plans have been approved to convert the distillery into a hotel and events venue.	
Also try	Clynelish, Glendullan, Glen Ord	
Availability	Very rare. Specialist retailers	
Price	£65 plus	

Malt	**CONVALMORE**	
Pronounced	*Conval-MORE*	
Distillery	Convalmore	
Website	www.malts.com	
Established	1984. Closed 1985.	
Status	Lost	
Main bottling	Rare Malts, Special Releases and independent bottlings	
Nose	Heather aroma with floral sweetness.	
Taste	Much fuller on the palate than the nose suggests.	
Finish	Warming, round and surprisingly long.	
Comments	After-dinner. A blending malt that is now lost. William Grant & Sons bought Convalmore in 1990 for warehousing capacity.	
Also try	Highland Park, Benrinnes, Longmorn	
Availability	Specialist retailers	
Price	£60 plus	

Malt	GLENCRAIG
Distillery	Glenburgie
Main bottling	Independents
Status	Lost
Nose	Fresh cut grass, mint chews and bananas.
Taste	Hint of spices, grassy oily notes, oak.
Finish	Long, oily and drying.
Comments	A sweet, creamy dram produced in Lomond stills at Glenburgie from 1956–81.
Also try	Mosstowie, Scapa, Inverleven
Availability	Very rare. Specialist retailers
Price	£100 plus

Malt	MOSSTOWIE
Pronounced	*Moss-TOW-ay*
Distillery	Miltonduff
Status	Lost
Main bottling	Independents
Comments	A real rarity. No tasting notes available.
Availability	Rare. Specialist retailers
Price	£83 plus

Malt	**PITTYVAICH**
Distillery	Pittyvaich
Website	www.malts.com
Established	1974. Closed 1993. Demolished 2002.
Status	Lost
Main bottling	Special Releases and independent bottlings
Nose	Olive-oily, then fruity, grassy with a suggestion of pineapple.
Taste	Appetising. Crisp, clean grass with sweet apple fruit. Sharp mineral mouthfeel with a trace of oiliness.
Finish	Short to medium. A very good aperitif whisky.
Comments	An interesting dram from a shortlived distillery built to fuel the success of Bell's blend in the 1970s.
Also try	Dufftown, Glen Spey, Speyburn
Availability	Rare. Specialist retailers
Price	£30 plus

The Highlands

FOUR distinct producing regions exist around Speyside at all points of the compass. From within them some 47 malts emanate (along with one grain whisky at Invergordon) in the northern region which extends from Dalwhinnie to Wick and consists of 16 distilleries, of which four no longer exist (Ben Wyvis, Glen Albyn, Glen Mhor and Millburn) and one is defunct (Brora). The remaining 11 distilleries are in rude health and are owned by a very international array of companies whose head offices are in countries as far apart as Bermuda, Thailand, India and Japan.

To the west there are two active distilleries at Oban and Fort William along with a lost distillery, Glenlochy, also in Fort William. Further to the north-west the micro-distillery at Loch Ewe represents an interesting means of undertaking small-scale production.

In the east there are five lost distilleries at Peterhead (Glenugie), Stonehaven (Glenury Royal), Montrose (Lochside) and Brechin (North Port/Brechin and Glenesk/Hillside). The active distilleries range from the coast of the Moray Firth (Macduff), through Deeside (Royal Lochnagar) and Aberdeenshire (Glen Garioch) to Angus (Fettercairn and Glencadam).

In the south the distilleries are located in Perthshire (Aberfeldy, Blair Athol, Edradour, Glenturret, Tullibardine), Stirlingshire and along the northern side of the imaginary old Highland Line which runs between Dumbarton and Dundee and effectively splits the Highland region from the Lowlands (Deanston, Glengoyne and Loch Lomond).

The northern and western malts are generally robust in nature with some maritime hints while the eastern and southern malts display more subtle characteristics which are all put to good use by the master blenders when creating some of the most popular Scotch whiskies. Glenturret's contribution to The Famous Grouse is inescapable to the visitor to Scotland as the distillery is home to the brand and is a popular tourist destination (www.thefamousgrouse.com).

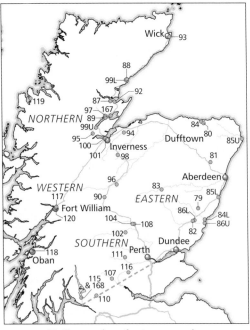

Distillery number refers to page number.
U = upper, L = lower

Similarly Tullibardine has been resurrected by new owners after a period of closure and is well situated at Blackford on the A9 in a large retail development which makes it an ideal stopping-off point when touring Scotland. Loch Lomond Distillery is particularly fascinating as it can produce pot-still malt whisky, patent-still grain whisky and patent-still malt whisky on site. The result is complete independence from outside suppliers of any of the ingredients required to produce the company's brands which include the popular supermarket blend, High Commissioner. The fact that the Scotch Whisky Association did not consider the malt whisky the distillery produces in its patent still to be worthy of official Scotch whisky classification is, we feel, an oversight as it means the process and technology can be duplicated overseas by other distillers.

Malt	FETTERCAIRN FIOR
Pronounced	*Fee-YAWR*
Distillery	Fettercairn LAURENCEKIRK AB30 1YB
Owner	United Spirits
Reception centre	01561 340205
Established	1824
Status	In production
Water source	Springs in the Grampians
Malt source	Commercial maltsters
Phenolic content	15 ppm
Casks	First-fill ex-bourbon
Annual output	2 million litres of alcohol
Stills	Wash: 2 Spirit: 2
Main bottling	No age statement, 42%
Nose	Rich. Crushed pear and toffee apple with cinnamon, vanilla and gooseberries. Orange rind, ginger and coriander.
Taste	Dark bitter chocolate, rich roast coffee beans, citrus fruits and truffles. Peat-smoke prickle, nutmeg and mint.
Finish	Hints of sherry trifle, marzipan and ripe pineapple. Fascinating.
Comments	Fettercairn is being rebranded and Fior is the result.
Also try	Deanston, Glenrothes, Tormore
Availability	Specialist retailers
Price	£20–25

Malt	**GLEN DEVERON**
Pronounced	*Glen DEV-erin*
Distillery	Macduff
	MACDUFF
	AB45 3JT
Owner	Bacardi
Established	1960
Status	In production
Water source	Local springs
Malt source	Commercial maltsters
Phenolic content	Unpeated
Casks	Refill and first-fill hogsheads and butts
Annual output	3.34 million litres of alcohol
Stills	Wash: 2
	Spirit: 3
Main bottling	10 years old, 40%
Nose	Candied toffee with fresh apple. Smooth, malty and fresh cereal base. After adding some water there are hints of almond and creamy oak.
Taste	Rich, creamy with chocolate overtones, cereal and fresh toasted oak. Medium-bodied.
Finish	Medium to long, dry with a subtle hint of sherry wood.
Comments	Used in the William Lawson blend and also bottled independently as Macduff.
Also try	Banff, Auchroisk, Glenglassaugh
Availability	Specialist retailers
Price	£25–30

Malt	**GLEN GARIOCH**
Pronounced	*Glen GEER-ay*
Distillery	Glen Garioch
	OLDMELDRUM
	AB51 0ES
Owner	Suntory
Reception centre	01651 873450
Website	www.glengarioch.com
Established	1797
Status	In production
Water source	Springs on Percock Hill
Malt source	Simpson's, Berwick-Upon-Tweed
Phenolic content	Unpeated
Casks	Ex-bourbon and sherry
Annual output	750,000 litres of alcohol
Stills	Wash: 1
	Spirit: 1
Main bottling	No age statement, 48%
Nose	Sweet vanilla and butterscotch with green apple and grapefruit.
Taste	Sweet with buttercream and vanilla. Then green apple and citrus.
Finish	Zesty and refreshing.
Comments	Repackaged and rebranded, Glen Garioch is worth searching out.
Also try	Oban, Craigellachie, Glenury Royal
Availability	Specialist retailers
Price	£28 plus

Malt	GLENCADAM
Distillery	Glencadam
	BRECHIN
	DD9 7PA
Owner	Angus Dundee Distillers plc
Reception centre	By appointment
Website	www.angusdundee.co.uk
Established	1825
Status	In production
Water source	Loch Lee
Malt source	Commercial maltsters
Phenolic content	Unpeated
Casks	Ex-bourbon
Annual output	1.5 million litres of alcohol
Stills	Wash: 1
	Spirit: 1
Main bottling	10 years old, 46%
Nose	Delicate, intense, grassy freshness and citrus tones with hints of spicy oak.
Taste	Rounded elegance. Clean, crisp citrus notes. Pleasing balance between natural sweetness and soft, spicy oak.
Finish	Long, soothing. Rich, clean, barley and gristy sweetness.
Comments	Now Brechin's only remaining distillery under British ownership.
Also try	Glenesk, North Port, Lochside
Availability	Widespread
Price	£25–30

Malt	ROYAL LOCHNAGAR
Pronounced	*Loch-na-GAAR*
Distillery	Royal Lochnagar
	BALLATER
	AB35 5TB
Owner	Diageo
Reception centre	01339 742700
Website	www.malts.com
Established	1845
Status	In production
Water source	Spring beneath the distillery
Malt source	Roseisle Maltings
Phenolic content	Unpeated
Casks	American and European oak
Annual output	400,000 litres of alcohol
Stills	Wash: 1
	Spirit: 1
Main bottling	12 years old, 40%
Nose	Planed wood, light toffee, boat varnish. Linseed oil behind and later a lychee-like acidity.
Taste	Medium-bodied. Pleasant; an initial sweetness is quickly overtaken by acidity.
Finish	Dry; medium-length, with an attractive lingering sandalwood aftertaste.
Comments	Queen Victoria's favourite tipple.
Also try	Dalmore, Macallan, Mortlach
Availability	Widespread
Price	£28 plus

Malt	**BANFF**
Distillery	Banff
Website	www.malts.com
Established	1863. Closed 1983.
Status	Lost
Main bottling	Rare Malts and independent bottlings
Nose	Full-bodied with plenty of orchard fruits and a hint of spice.
Taste	Well balanced with sultanas, some sherry notes and spice.
Finish	Long-lasting, oaky and spicey.
Comments	A lost distillery that was plagued with fires.
Also try	Mortlach, Balmenach, Dailuaine
Availability	Rare. Specialist retailers
Price	£85 plus

Malt	**GLENESK**
Distillery	Glenesk
Website	www.malts,com
Established	1897. Closed 1985.
Status	Lost
Main bottling	Rare Malts and independent bottlings
Nose	A delicate hint of sweetness, barley sugar and dried fruits.
Taste	Quite full, round and sweet, well balanced, again dried fruits and herbs.
Finish	Long, lingering, warming.
Comments	Also bottled as Hillside for a period of time.
Also try	North Port, Glencadam, Lochside
Availability	Very rare. Specialist retailers
Price	£70 plus

Malt	**GLENUGIE**
Pronounced	*Glen-OO-gee*
Distillery	Glenugie
Established	c.1831. Closed 1968.
Status	Lost
Main bottling	Rare Malts and independent bottlings
Nose	Hint of ripe fruit sweetness and a rich warmth.
Taste	Initial trace of sweetness. Firm, smoky and malty.
Finish	Subtle and dry.
Comments	Barely a vestige remains of this Peterhead distillery.
Also try	Glenury-Royal, Glen Deveron, Glen Garioch
Availability	Specialist retailers
Price	£95 plus

Malt	**GLENURY ROYAL**
Pronounced	*Glen-YOU-ray*
Distillery	Glenury Royal
Website	www.malts.com
Established	c.1825. Closed 1985.
Status	Lost
Main bottling	Independents
Nose	Light hint of smoke with a dry, fruity, fresh aroma.
Taste	Light-bodied, dry and smoky.
Finish	The smoke continues on a long, dry, rich finish.
Comments	Established by Captain Robert Barclay Allardice, the first man to walk 1,000 miles in 1,000 consecutive hours for a wager of 1,000 guineas in 1809.
Also try	Glenugie, Glen Garioch, Glen Deveron
Availability	Very rare. Specialist retailers
Price	£70 plus

Malt	**LOCHSIDE**
Distillery	Lochside
Established	1957. Closed 1996. Demolished 2005.
Status	Lost
Main bottling	Independents
Nose	Light, aromatic with a delicate sweetness and a gentle background of dryness.
Taste	Initially sweet, medium-dry with a lingering, stimulating mouthfeel.
Finish	Long and gentle.
Comments	The last owner's bottlings from this distillery can fetch £150 at auction.
Also try	Glencadam, North Port, Glenesk
Availability	Rare. Specialist retailers
Price	£35 plus

Malt	**NORTH PORT**
Distillery	North Port
Website	www.malts.com
Established	c.1820. Closed 1983.
Status	Lost
Main bottling	Rare Malts and independent bottlings
Nose	A light, sweet pronounced aroma with an astringent background. Some spice and a hint of smoke.
Taste	Starts sweet but quickly fades to spirit.
Finish	A pleasant, sharp tangy finish.
Comments	Pre-dinner with just a little water. Also bottled as Brechin.
Also try	Glencadam, Glenesk, Lochside
Availability	Rare. Specialist retailers
Price	£60 plus

Malt	BALBLAIR
Pronounced	*Baal-BLAIR*
Distillery	Balblair
	TAIN
	IV19 1LB
Owner	Thai Beverages
Website	www.balblair.com
Established	1790
Status	In production
Water source	Allt Dearg Burn
Malt source	Local commercial maltsters
Phenolic content	1.5 ppm maximum
Casks	First- and second-fill ex-bourbon and refill ex-sherry
Annual output	1.36 million litres of alcohol
Stills	Wash: 1
	Spirit: 1
Main bottling	1997 distillation, 43%
Nose	Fused with the aromas of pineapple, apricot and lemon.
Taste	Hints of oak, spice, raisins and sweet vanilla.
Finish	Long and lingering, creamy and smooth.
Comments	One of the five malts from the Inver House stable.
Also try	Glen Garioch, Oban, Old Pulteney
Availability	Specialist retailers
Price	£25–30

Malt	CLYNELISH
Pronounced	*KLYNE-leesh*
Distillery	Clynelish
	BRORA
	KW9 6LR
Owner	Diageo
Reception centre	01408 623003
Website	www.malts.com
Established	1967
Status	In production
Water source	Clynemilton Burn
Malt source	Glen Ord Maltings
Phenolic content	Unpeated
Casks	Ex-bourbon
Annual output	4.2 million litres of alcohol
Stills	Wash: 3
	Spirit: 3
Main bottling	14 years old, 46%
Nose	Light candle wax with some sugar, faint floral fragrance.
Taste	Pleasant, creamy mouthfeel with maritime overtones. Light to medium-bodied.
Finish	Some salt, dryish yet an attractive, even slightly bitter finish.
Comments	Next door to silent Brora yet utterly different.
Also try	Balvenie, Glen Ord, Linkwood
Availability	Rare. Specialist retailers
Price	£25 plus

Malt	**DALMORE**
Pronounced	*Daal-MORE*
Distillery	Dalmore
	ALNESS
	IV17 0UT
Owner	United Spirits
Reception centre	By appointment. 01349 882362
Website	www.thedalmore.com
Established	1839
Status	In production
Water source	Loch Kildermorie
Malt source	Bairds of Inverness
Phenolic content	Unpeated
Casks	American and European oak
Annual output	3.1 million litres of alcohol
Stills	Wash: 4
	Spirit: 4
Main bottling	12 years old, 40%
Nose	Firm, positive, elegant. Citrus fruits and crushed almonds, subtle hints of marzipan and chocolate.
Taste	Intense, warming mouthfeel with citrus, sherry and exotic spices.
Finish	Long and lingering.
Comments	A magnificent post-dinner malt.
Also try	Mortlach, Macallan, Royal Lochnagar
Availability	Widespread
Price	£33 plus

Malt	DALWHINNIE
Pronounced	*Daal-WHINN-ay*
Distillery	Dalwhinnie
	DALWHINNIE
	PH19 1AA
Owner	Diageo
Reception centre	01540 672219
Website	www.malts.com
Established	1897
Status	In production
Water source	Allt an t'Sluie Burn
Malt source	Roseisle Maltings
Phenolic content	Lightly peated
Casks	Ex-bourbon, matured offsite in Central Scotland
Annual output	2 million litres of alcohol
Stills	Wash: 1
	Spirit: 1
Main bottling	15 years old, 43%
Nose	Big, crisp, dry and very aromatic with hints of heather and peat.
Taste	Heather-honey sweetness and vanilla followed by deeper citrus-fruit and hints of malted bread.
Finish	Long, lingering, surprisingly intense; starts sweetly, then gives way to smoke, peat and malt.
Comments	Scotland's highest distillery (356 m/1168 ft)
Also try	Balvenie, Glenlivet, Linkwood
Availability	Everywhere
Price	£30 plus

Malt	DRUMGUISH
Pronounced	*Drum-OO-ish*
Distillery	Speyside
	KINGUSSIE
	PH21 1NS
Owner	Speyside Distillers Co Ltd
Reception centre	By appointment
Website	www.speysidedistillery.co.uk
Established	1990
Status	In production
Water source	River Tromie
Malt source	Local commercial maltsters
Phenolic content	Less than 5 ppm
Casks	Ex-bourbon and sherry refills
Annual output	500,000 litres of alcohol
Stills	Wash: 1
	Spirit: 1
Main bottling	No age statement, 40%
Nose	Soft and medium-sweet. Quite fresh with a slight menthol character, gently peated with a slight earthy touch.
Taste	Medium-dry, minty, with good body and a firm, but gentle, dark, earthy smokiness.
Finish	Of good length, almost dry with a light, sweet character.
Comments	Although close to the Spey, this distillery is far removed from the traditional low-lying Speyside distilling area.
Also try	Cardhu, Glen Grant, Speyside
Availability	Specialist retailers
Price	£15

Malt	**GLENMORANGIE**
Pronounced	*Glen-MORANGE-ay*
Distillery	Glenmorangie
	TAIN
	IV19 1PZ
Owner	LVMH
Reception centre	01862 892477
Website	www.glenmorangie.com
Established	1843
Status	In production
Water source	Tarlogie Springs
Malt source	Commercial maltsters
Phenolic content	Unpeated
Casks	First and second refill ex-bourbon with some other woods for finishing
Annual output	4.5 million litres of alcohol
Stills	Wash: 6
	Spirit: 6
Main bottling	10 years old, 40%
Nose	Orchard-fruit aroma. Fresh, sweet with citrus and floral overtones.
Taste	Medium-bodied with a sweet, fresh, orchard-fruit taste and some vanilla and almond overtones.
Finish	Satisfying and refreshing.
Comments	A very popular malt, particularly in Scotland.
Also try	Balblair, Old Pulteney, Teaninich
Availability	Everywhere
Price	£30

Malt	OLD PULTENEY
Pronounced	*Old PULT-nay*
Distillery	Pulteney
	WICK
	KW1 5BA
Owner	Thai Beverages
Reception centre	01955 602371
Website	www.oldpulteney.com
Established	1826
Status	In production
Water source	Mains water from the Loch of Hempriggs
Phenolic content	Unpeated
Casks	Ex-bourbon and sherry
Stills	Wash: 1
	Spirit: 1
Main bottling	12 years old, 40%
Nose	Medium to high intensity, dry with a hint of sea air.
Taste	Dry, medium-bodied and smooth.
Finish	Clean and faintly salty with a slight sherry note.
Comments	An increasingly popular Highland malt.
Also try	Balblair, Glen Garioch, Cragganmore
Availability	Everywhere
Price	£25 plus

Malt	ROYAL BRACKLA
Distillery	Royal Brackla
	NAIRN
	IV12 5QY
Owner	Bacardi
Established	c.1812
Status	In production
Water source	Cursack Springs
Malt source	Commercial maltsters
Phenolic content	Unpeated
Casks	Refill American oak casks
Annual output	4.03 million litres of alcohol
Stills	Wash: 2
	Spirit: 2
Main bottling	10 years old, 40%
Nose	Light, fresh, floral nose.
Taste	Medium-bodied, leafy, with well-rounded floral character. Fruity and spicy.
Finish	Long, malty finish with a hint of oak.
Comments	One of the signature malts in Dewar's blends.
Also try	Clynelish, Glen Elgin, Cardhu
Availability	Specialist retailers
Price	£28–32

Malt	THE SINGLETON OF GLEN ORD
Distillery	Glen Ord MUIR OF ORD IV6 7UJ
Owner	Diageo
Reception centre	01463 872004
Website	www.malts.com
Established	1838
Status	In production
Water source	Nan Eun and Nam Bonnach Lochs
Malt source	Glen Ord Maltings
Phenolic content	Lightly peated
Casks	Fresh and refill ex-sherry butts and refill hogsheads
Annual output	3.4 million litres of alcohol
Stills	Wash: 3 Spirit: 3
Main bottling	12 years old, 40%
Nose	Beautifully deep nose with a tinge of dryness and mixed spice.
Taste	Good depth, very smooth and slightly smoky.
Finish	Delicious, long-lasting, very smooth and moreish.
Comments	Now available direct from the distillery.
Also try	BenRiach, Glen Elgin, Royal Brackla
Availability	Specialist retailers
Price	£30 plus

Malt	SPEYSIDE
Distillery	Speyside
	KINGUSSIE
	PH21 1NS
Owner	Speyside Distillers Co Ltd
Reception centre	By appointment
Website	www.speysidedistillery.co.uk
Established	1990
Status	In production
Water source	River Tromie
Malt source	Local commercial maltsters
Phenolic content	Less than 5 ppm
Casks	Ex-bourbon and sherry refills
Annual output	500,000 litres of alcohol
Stills	Wash: 1
	Spirit: 1
Main bottling	12 years old, 40%
Nose	Clean, delicate and balanced with a toasted barley aroma.
Taste	A slightly peaty flavour gives way to creamy ripples of hazelnut.
Finish	Lingering hints of vanilla and toffee. Smooth and satisfying.
Comments	The closest Highland distillery to the River Spey.
Also try	Drumguish, Glengoyne, Tamdhu
Availability	Widespread
Price	£25–30

Malt	TEANINICH
Pronounced	*Tee-ninn-ich*
Distillery	Teaninich
	ALNESS
	IV17 0XB
Owner	Diageo
Website	www.malts.com
Established	1817
Status	In production
Water source	Dairywell Spring
Malt source	Glen Ord Maltings
Phenolic content	Unpeated
Casks	Refill ex-bourbon hogsheads with some ex-sherry butts
Annual output	4 million litres of alcohol
Stills	Wash: 3
	Spirit: 3
Main bottling	Manager's Choice and independent bottlings
Nose	Fresh, light touch of smoke with a hint of fruit and a delicate sweetness.
Taste	Medium-bodied with a gentle oakiness.
Finish	Smooth and long.
Comments	One of Diageo's main blending malts.
Also try	Balblair, Oban, Old Pulteney
Availability	Specialist retailers
Price	£35 plus

Malt	TOMATIN
Pronounced	*Tom-AA-tin*
Distillery	Tomatin
	TOMATIN
	IV13 7YT
Owner	Marubeni Europe Ltd
Reception centre	01463 248144
Website	www.tomatin.com
Established	1897
Status	In production
Water source	Allt na Frithe Burn
Malt source	Commercial maltsters
Phenolic content	Unpeated and peated (2–5 ppm)
Casks	Ex-bourbon, refill hogsheads and ex-sherry butts
Annual output	5 million litres of alcohol
Stills	Wash: 12
	Spirit: 11
Main bottling	12 years old, 40%
Nose	A complex bouquet contains rich malt and fruity aromas with a hint of peatiness.
Taste	A combination of attractive flavours — a balance of apples, pears and malt with a gentle hint of nuttiness enhanced by the subtle nuance of sherry wood.
Finish	Smooth, sweet and satisfying.
Comments	One of Scotland's largest malt distilleries.
Also try	Dalwhinnie, Speyside, Glen Mhor
Availability	Specialist retailers
Price	£20–30

Malt	**BEN WYVIS**
Pronounced	*Ben Wiviss*
Distillery	Ben Wyvis
Established	1965. Closed 1977. Now dismantled.
Status	Lost
Main bottling	37 years old, 44%
Nose	Soft marzipan, parma violets and floral vanilla against an oaky background.
Taste	Elegant and finessed. A hint of liquorice and exotic spice.
Finish	Sumptuous, rich and well-balanced.
Comments	The stills were reinstalled at Glen Gyle Distillery in Campbeltown.
Also try	Dalmore, Mortlach, Dailuaine
Availability	Very rare. Specialist retailers
Price	£750 plus

Malt	**BRORA**
Pronounced	*BROAR-ah*
Distillery	Brora
Website	www.malts.com
Established	1819. Closed 1983.
Status	Lost
Main bottling	Rare Malts, Special Releases and independent bottlings
Nose	Wet salt and dry, grassy woodsmoke.
Taste	Cloying but refined mouthfeel, smooth oak and a citrus edge. Full, fleshy fruits with some smoke.
Finish	Rich, long, nutty and smoky.
Comments	Remarkable, almost Islay-like Highland malt.
Also try	Caol Ila, Ardbeg, Port Ellen
Availability	Rare. Specialist retailers
Price	£85 plus

Malt	**GLEN ALBYN**
Pronounced	*Glen AAL-binn*
Distillery	Glen Albyn
Website	www.malts.com
Established	c.1846. Closed 1983. Dismantled 1986.
Status	Lost
Main bottling	Rare Malts and independent bottlings

Nose	Aromatic, scented and sweet. With water, acid drops appear against a trace of black coffee.
Taste	Rich mouthfeel, light but firm-bodied, smooth, drying on the palate.
Finish	Bitter, peppy, but not unattractive.
Comments	Tastes its age, but not over the hill.
Also try	Glen Mhor, Glenfarclas, Glen Ord
Availability	Specialist retailers
Price	£80 plus

Malt	**GLEN MHOR**
Pronounced	*Glen VAWRR*
Distillery	Glen Mhor
Website	www.malts.com
Established	1892. Closed 1983. Dismantled 1986.
Status	Lost
Main bottling	Rare Malts and independent bottlings.

Nose	Sweet, almond-like with a trace of coconut. With water, a trace of strawberry jam emerges.
Taste	Light, cloying and zesty. Sweet with a trace of dry peat. Citrus overtones and drying.
Finish	Medium-length. Acid drops. Peppermint tea. Soothing.
Comments	Novelist Neil Gunn's favourite malt.
Also try	Glen Albyn, Millburn, Royal Brackla
Availability	Specialist retailers
Price	£40 plus

Malt	MILLBURN
Distillery	Millburn
Website	www.malts.com
Established	c.1807. Closed 1985.
Status	Lost
Main bottling	Rare Malts and independent bottlings
Nose	Rich aroma with a medium sweetness and a hint of smoke.
Taste	Medium- to full-bodied, a touch of fruit.
Finish	Long, sweet and dry.
Comments	The distillery is now a restaurant.
Also try	Glen Albyn, Glen Mhor, Royal Brackla
Availability	Specialist retailers
Price	£85 plus

Malt	**ABERFELDY**
Pronounced	*Aber-FELL-day*
Distillery	Aberfeldy
	ABERFELDY
	PH15 2EB
Owner	Bacardi
Reception centre	01887 822010
Website	www.dewarswow.com
Established	1896
Status	In production
Water source	Pitilie Burn
Malt source	Commercial maltsters
Phenolic content	Unpeated
Casks	Refill American hogsheads and some refill European wood
Annual output	2.85 million litres of alcohol
Stills	Wash: 2
	Spirit: 2
Main bottling	12 years old, 40%
Nose	Rich, rounded and full with heather, honey, notes of sweet pineapple, butter toffee, toast, cereal and vanilla.
Taste	Deep, sweet golden syrup and honey followed by spices and orange peel. Medium- to full-bodied.
Finish	Perfume characteristics become spicy with a hint of orange peel and a dry finish.
Comments	The bedrock malt of the Dewar's brand.
Also try	Blair Athol, Edradour, Ben Nevis
Availability	Widespread
Price	£28–32

Malt	BALLECHIN
Pronounced	*Bal-ECH-inn*
Distillery	Edradour
	PITLOCHRY
	PH16 5JP
Owner	The Signatory Vintage Scotch Whisky Co Ltd
Reception centre	01796 472095
Website	www.edradour.com
Established	1825
Status	In production
Water source	Springs on Moulin Moor
Malt source	Bairds of Pencaitland and Inverness
Phenolic content	50–60 ppm
Casks	Ex-bourbon and sherry
Annual output	100,000 litres of alcohol
Stills	Wash: 1
	Spirit: 1
Main bottling	Release no 4, 46%
Nose	Very heavy smoke and soft fruit.
Taste	Peat smoke calmed by the richness of the Oloroso, then soft berry fruits.
Finish	Long and very satisfying.
Comments	A highly peated malt distilled since 2003 and matured in Oloroso casks. Recreates the Victorian whisky made at nearby Ballechin Distillery, now long gone. 25% of Edradour output is Ballechin.
Also try	Ardbeg, Laphroaig, Port Charlotte
Availability	Specialist retailers
Price	£55 plus

Malt	**BLAIR ATHOL**
Pronounced	*Blair AATH-ol*
Distillery	Blair Athol
	PITLOCHRY
	PH16 5LY
Owner	Diageo
Reception centre	01796 482003
Website	www.malts.com
Established	1798
Status	In production
Water source	Allt Dour
Malt source	Glen Ord Maltings
Phenolic content	Unpeated
Casks	Ex-bourbon
Annual output	2.5 million litres of alcohol
Stills	Wash: 2
	Spirit: 2
Main bottling	Manager's Choice and independent bottlings
Nose	Appetising. Candied lemon peel. Nutty, sweetish. Sherry. Rich, giving way to sweeter, cake-like aromas.
Taste	Medium- to full-bodied. Creamy. Malty. Sweet, moist, ginger cake. Toasted nuts.
Finish	Spicy. Scenty. Medium-length and warming as it travels down.
Comments	Most of the production finds its way into the Bell's blends.
Also try	Aberfeldy, Edradour, Longmorn
Availability	Specialist retailers
Price	£27 plus

Loch Lomond Distillery
stillhouse

Malt	CRAIGLODGE
Distillery	Loch Lomond
	ALEXANDRIA
	G83 0TL
Owner	Loch Lomond Distillery Ltd
Website	www.lochlomonddistillery.com
Established	1966
Status	In production
Water source	Borehole aquifers and Loch Lomond
Malt source	Commercial grain dealers
Phenolic content	20 ppm
Casks	Ex-bourbon casks
Annual output	4 million litres of alcohol
Stills	Wash: 2
	Spirit: 4
Main bottling	4 years old, 45%
Nose	Estery with a peaty overlay.
Taste	Well-balanced mixture of peat, fruit and malt.
Finish	Malty notes with lingering balanced peat.
Comments	One of the three peated malts produced by Loch Lomond.
Also try	Ardmore, Glen Scotia, Bowmore
Availability	Specialist retailers and at the distillery
Price	£28

Malt	CROFTENGEA
Pronounced	*Kroft-enn-GEE*
Distillery	Loch Lomond
	ALEXANDRIA
	G83 0TL
Owner	Loch Lomond Distillery Ltd
Website	www.lochlomonddistillery.com
Established	1966
Status	In production
Water source	Borehole aquifers and Loch Lomond
Malt source	Commercial grain dealers
Phenolic content	35 ppm
Casks	Ex-bourbon casks
Annual output	4 million litres of alcohol
Stills	Wash: 2
	Spirit: 4
Main bottling	Distilled 1997, 45%
Nose	Heavy, smoky, peaty.
Taste	Intense peat and smoky flavours moderated by fruity esters.
Finish	Long, lingering, oily peat smoke.
Comments	An alternative to Islay?
Also try	Ardbeg, Laqavulin, Kilchoman
Availability	Specialist retailers and at the distillery
Price	£29

Malt	DEANSTON
Distillery	Deanston
	DOUNE
	FK16 6AG
Owner	C L Financial
Reception centre	01786 841422
Website	www.deanstonmalt.com
Established	1965–6
Status	In production
Water source	River Teith
Malt source	Commercial maltsters
Phenolic content	1–2 ppm
Casks	Fresh and refill sherry butts and hogsheads, fresh and refill ex-bourbon, refill ex-whisky barrels, butts and hogsheads plus de-charred, re-charred casks
Annual output	3 million litres of alcohol
Stills	Wash: 2
	Spirit: 2
Main bottling	12 years old, 40%
Nose	Fresh, floral, citrus fruit laden with a honeycomb maltiness.
Taste	Barley sugar, creamy toffee, orange with hints of ginger. Medium-bodied.
Finish	Long and balanced, spiced honey flavours.
Comments	Interesting dram from a distillery created from a converted cotton mill built in 1785.
Also try	Glen Deveron, Glenrothes, Tullibardine
Availability	Widespread
Price	£30–35

Malt	**EDRADOUR**
Pronounced	*Edd-ra-DOW-er*
Distillery	Edradour
	PITLOCHRY
	PH16 5JP
Owner	The Signatory Vintage Scotch Whisky Co Ltd
Reception centre	01796 472095
Website	www.edradour.com
Established	1825
Status	In production
Water source	Springs on Moulin Moor
Malt source	Bairds of Pencaitland and Inverness
Phenolic content	Unpeated
Casks	Ex-bourbon and sherry
Annual output	100,000 litres of alcohol
Stills	Wash: 1
	Spirit: 1
Main bottling	10 years old, 40%
Nose	Peppermint, sugared almond, hint of sherry, spicy-smoky notes.
Taste	Remarkably creamy texture for a relatively light malt. Minty-clean, creamy, malty.
Finish	Mellow and warming.
Comments	Bottled at the distillery. New warehousing will mature all future stocks on site. Private tours and tasting bar.
Also try	Aberfeldy, Blair Athol, Glenturret
Availability	Specialist retailers
Price	£30 plus

Malt	GLEN DOUGLAS
Distillery	Loch Lomond
	ALEXANDRIA
	G83 0TL
Owner	Loch Lomond Distillery Ltd
Website	www.lochlomonddistillery.com
Established	1966
Status	In production
Water source	Borehole aquifers and Loch Lomond
Malt source	Commercial grain dealers
Phenolic content	Unpeated
Casks	Ex-bourbon casks
Annual output	4 million litres of alcohol
Stills	Wash: 2
	Spirit: 4
Main bottling	5 years old, 45%
Nose	Complex apricot notes.
Taste	Soft, complex almost winey fruit palate.
Finish	Delicate yet complex.
Comments	One of the six malts that Loch Lomond produces.
Also try	Bladnoch, Caperdonich, Glenkinchie
Availability	Specialist retailers and at the distillery
Price	£26

Malt	GLENGOYNE
Distillery	Glengoyne
	KILLEARN
	G63 9LB
Owner	Ian Macleod & Co Ltd
Reception centre	01360 550254
Website	www.glengoyne.com
Established	c.1833
Status	In production
Water source	Distillery Burn from Campsie Fells
Malt source	Simpson's, Berwick-Upon-Tweed
Phenolic content	Unpeated
Casks	Ex-sherry and refill casks
Annual output	1.1 million litres of alcohol
Stills	Wash: 1
	Spirit: 2
Main bottling	10 years old, 40%
Nose	Sweet, with toffee and popcorn aromas. Slightly nutty, with fresh green apples coming through.
Taste	Warm mouthfeel. Clean. Green apples and grass with a hint of sweet liquorice. After the addition of water it is sweeter with hints of linseed oil and almonds.
Finish	Sweet and malty.
Comments	A fine malt from a beautifully situated distillery.
Also try	Auchentoshan, Loch Lomond, Littlemill
Availability	Widespread
Price	£25 plus

Malt	GLENTURRET
Distillery	Glenturret
	CRIEFF
	PH7 4HA
Owner	Edrington Group
Reception centre	01764 656565
Website	www.thefamousgrouse.com
Established	1775
Status	In production
Water source	Mains water from Loch Turret
Malt source	Simpson's, Berwick-Upon-Tweed
Phenolic content	Unpeated and up to 150 ppm for blending fillings
Casks	Refill ex-sherry Spanish and American oak and small proportion of ex-bourbon
Annual output	300,000 litres of alcohol
Stills	Wash: 1
	Spirit: 1
Main bottling	10 years old, 40%
Nose	Spicy citrus with a mild peat aroma.
Taste	Very soft, mature orange zest/vanilla spirit.
Finish	Dry, light and fairly short with cereal overtones at the back.
Comments	The home of the Famous Grouse brand.
Also try	Blair Athol, Aberfeldy, Edradour
Availability	Specialist retailers
Price	£27 plus

Malt	INCHFAD
Pronounced	*Inch-FAAD*
Distillery	Loch Lomond
	ALEXANDRIA
	G83 0TL
Owner	Loch Lomond Distillery Ltd
Website	www.lochlomonddistillery.com
Established	1966
Status	In production
Water source	Borehole aquifers and Loch Lomond
Malt source	Commercial grain dealers
Phenolic content	Unpeated
Casks	Ex-bourbon casks
Annual output	4 million litres of alcohol
Stills	Wash: 2
	Spirit: 4
Main bottling	Distilled 2001, 45%
Nose	Firm and malty.
Taste	Full-bodied, malty, sweet fruit and vanilla overtones.
Finish	Malty vanilla with lingering fruit.
Comments	One of Loch Lomond's many malt expressions.
Also try	Blair Athol, Edradour, Glenturret
Availability	Specialist retailers and at the distillery
Price	£26

Malt	INCHMOAN
Distillery	Loch Lomond
	ALEXANDRIA
	G83 0TL
Owner	Loch Lomond Distillery Ltd
Website	www.lochlomonddistillery.com
Established	1966
Status	In production
Water source	Borehole aquifers and Loch Lomond
Malt source	Commercial grain dealers
Phenolic content	30 ppm
Casks	Ex-bourbon casks
Annual output	4 million litres of alcohol
Stills	Wash: 2
	Spirit: 4
Main bottling	4 years old, 45%
Nose	Light and surprisingly peaty.
Taste	Clean, solid malty tones with intense peat.
Finish	Clean, light but peaty.
Comments	Another peated expression from Loch Lomond.
Also try	Croftengea, Bowmore, Kilchoman
Availability	Specialist retailers and at the distillery
Price	£28

Malt	INCHMURRIN
Distillery	Loch Lomond
	ALEXANDRIA
	G83 0TL
Owner	Loch Lomond Distillery Ltd
Website	www.lochlomonddistillery.com
Established	1966
Status	In production
Water source	Borehole aquifers and Loch Lomond
Malt source	Commercial grain dealers
Phenolic content	Unpeated
Casks	Ex-bourbon casks
Annual output	4 million litres of alcohol
Stills	Wash: 2
	Spirit: 4
Main bottling	12 years old, 40%
Nose	Sweet and light.
Taste	Light, pleasantly oily and nutty.
Finish	Light with lingering oaky, vanilla notes.
Comments	Pre-dinner. Try chilling it and taking it straight.
Also try	Bladnoch, Auchentoshan, Glengoyne
Availability	Specialist retailers and at the distillery
Price	£20

Malt	LOCH LOMOND
Distillery	Loch Lomond
	ALEXANDRIA
	G83 0TL
Owner	Loch Lomond Distillery Ltd
Website	www.lochlomonddistillery.com
Established	1966
Status	In production
Water source	Borehole aquifers and Loch Lomond
Malt source	Commercial grain dealers
Phenolic content	Unpeated and peated
Casks	Ex-bourbon casks
Annual output	4 million litres of alcohol
Stills	Wash: 2
	Spirit: 4
Main bottling	No age statement, 40%
Nose	Mellow, slightly peaty nose, with a hint of brandy butter.
Taste	Light-bodied. Sweet, smokey, with hints of finest Madeira wine with a long, mellow finish and echoes of a raisiny Xmas pudding.
Finish	Quite quick, but mellow.
Comments	The signature malt from a unique distillery which also produces grain whisky.
Also try	Braeval, Glengoyne, Auchentoshan
Availability	Specialist retailers and at the distillery
Price	£20 plus

Malt	TULLIBARDINE
Pronounced	*Tully-BAAR-din*
Distillery	Tullibardine
	BLACKFORD
	PH4 1QG
Owner	Tullibardine Ltd
Reception centre	01764 682252
Website	www.tullibardine.com
Established	1949
Status	In production
Water source	Danny Burn on Ochil Hills
Malt source	Commercial maltsters
Phenolic content	Unpeated
Casks	First-fill ex-bourbon and ex-sherry hogsheads
Annual output	2.7 million litres of alcohol
Stills	Wash: 2
	Spirit: 2
Main bottling	No age statement, 40%
Nose	Youthful barley with light citrus notes, a touch of candied fruit and even a hint of mint.
Taste	Initial burst of flavours of barley, lemon and vanilla. Addition of water allows these aromas to come through.
Finish	Clean and crisp.
Comments	Another resurrected distillery now in rude health.
Also try	Deanston, Blair Athol, Aberfeldy
Availability	Specialist retailers
Price	£25 plus

Malt	BEN NEVIS
Distillery	Ben Nevis
	FORT WILLIAM
	PH33 6TJ
Owner	Nikka Distillers
Reception centre	01397 702476
Website	www.bennevisdistillery.com
Established	1825
Status	In production
Water source	Allt a Mhullin on Ben Nevis
Malt source	Commercial maltsters
Casks	Ex-bourbon and sherry
Annual output	2 million litres of alcohol
Stills	Wash: 2
	Spirit: 2
Main bottling	10 years old, 46%
Nose	Sweet, malty bouquet with rich hints of smoke and vanilla.
Taste	Coats the palate firmly. Rich, full-bodied. Aromatic.
Finish	Delicious long length of finish.
Comments	Fort William's only surviving distillery.
Also try	Aberfeldy, Glencadam, Scapa
Availability	Widespread
Price	£25–30

Malt	OBAN
Distillery	Oban
	OBAN
	PA34 5NH
Owner	Diageo
Reception centre	01631 572004
Website	www.malts.com
Established	1794
Status	In production
Water source	Loch Gleann a'Bhearraidh
Malt source	Roseisle Maltings
Phenolic content	Lightly peated
Casks	Refill American hogsheads
Annual output	700,000 litres of alcohol
Stills	Wash: 1
	Spirit: 1
Main bottling	14 years old, 43%
Nose	Rich sweetness and fruits — oranges, lemons and pears, with sea-salt and peaty smokiness.
Taste	Ful-bodied mouth-filling dried figs and honey-sweet spices followed by a smoky malty dryness.
Finish	Long, smooth and sweet with oak wood, dryness and a grain of salt.
Comments	A great place to visit when in Oban.
Also try	Ben Nevis, Bowmorc, Old Pulteney
Availability	Widespread
Price	£33 plus

Malt	SPIRIT OF LOCH EWE
Distillery	Loch Ewe
	AULTBEA
	IV22 2HU
Owner	John Clotworthy
Reception centre	Drumchork Lodge Hotel
	01445 731242
Website	www.lochewedistillery.co.uk
Established	2006
Status	In production
Water source	Mains water
Malt source	Simpson's, Berwick-Upon-Tweed
Phenolic content	Unpeated
Casks	2, 3 and 4-gallon bespoke casks with some Spanish Oloroso 5-litre casks
Annual output	Up to 600 litres of alcohol
Stills	Wash: 1
	Spirit: 1
Main bottling	10 cl, no age statement
Comments	Due to the low-volume production levels, each cask produced varies and no tasting notes are available at present.
Availability	Only from Drumchork Lodge Hotel
Price	£15 (10 cl) and £75 (50 cl)

Malt	GLENLOCHY
Distillery	Glenlochy
Website	www.malts.com
Established	1898. Closed 1983.
Status	Lost
Main bottling	Independent bottlings
Nose	Light and aromatic with a hint of sweetness and fruit.
Taste	Light, spicy flavour.
Finish	Fairly quick finish.
Comments	Glenlochy's distinctive pagoda remains but the malt is gradually disappearing.
Also try	Oban, Tobermory, Ben Nevis
Availability	Very rare. Specialist retailers
Price	£95 plus

The Lowlands

THIS region can only boast five working malt distilleries but is the largest in terms of grain whisky output with four of Scotland's six active grain distilleries. The central belt was the grain-distilling centre of Scotland as the 18th- and 19th-century Haig and Stein dynasties established and developed their businesses. Their huge Clackmannanshire distilleries produced pot-still grain spirit in vast, shallow stills that were flash-fired to distill rapidly. The result was commercially successful but the product was vile. The main market for it was England where it was rectified into gin to satisfy the thirst of the masses. Robert Stein's invention of the continuous still in 1826 (see Chapter 2) ushered in a new era of whisky distilling that gained the industry its worldwide status today. Nowadays grain distilling in this area is based in Fife at Cameron Bridge where all of Diageo's white spirit production takes place.

Edinburgh once boasted a large number of malt and grain distilleries but only the venerable North British grain distillery survives to this day. If you want to have a whisky experience in the capital then you will have to visit the Scotch Whisky Experience at the top of the Royal Mile, just before the Castle Esplanade (www.whisky-heritage.co.uk).

The Lowlands have also been home to many fine malt distilleries of which the present-day survivors are Glenkinchie, Bladnoch and Auchentoshan while recent losses have been Rosebank, Moffat, Inverleven, Kinclaith, Ladyburn and Littlemill. The two other active distilleries are relatively new with Ailsa Bay replacing Ladyburn at William Grant & Sons' Girvan complex, and the beautiful Daftmill Distillery in Fife which has been created by the Cuthbert family at their farm of the same name. Ailsa Bay is unlikely ever to be available on the market and we have therefore not listed it here. Daftmill will be available when it is considered ready and accordingly as much detail has been given as possible.

Stylistically Lowland malts were usually triple-distilled to create a lighter, more floral, estery and aromatic spirit. Only Auchentoshan continues with this practice which is

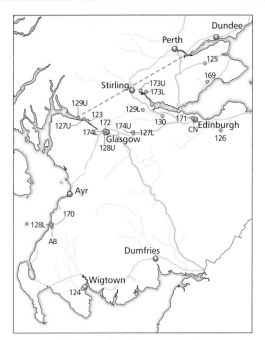

Distillery number refers to page number.
U = upper, L = lower, AB = Ailsa Bay, CN = Caledonian

now largely confined to Ireland. A new distillery is being planned close to Rosebank, so malt whisky distilling might yet return to Falkirk.

Glenkinchie has an excellent visitor centre while Bladnoch in Galloway operates on an entirely different scale and also functions as a community events venue during the Wigtown Book Festival every September. Although output is only 8,000 litres per week, the distillery warehouses 40,000 casks for other customers and operates an online Forum where members can buy unique bottlings of other malts. Both activities bring in vital income for what is a very hands-on operation run by a small, loyal team. The picturesque farm distillery at Annan is due to be resurrected in late 2011 after a £3.5 million investment from its new owners.

Malt	AUCHENTOSHAN
Pronounced	*OCH-in-TOSH-inn*
Distillery	Auchentoshan
	DALMUIR
	G81 4SJ
Owner	Suntory
Reception centre	01389 878561
Website	www.auchentoshan.co.uk
Established	1823
Status	In production
Water source	Loch Katrine for process, Kilpatrick Hills for cooling
Malt source	Commercial maltsters
Phenolic content	Unpeated
Casks	Ex-bourbon barrels with some sherry hogsheads and butts
Annual output	1.6 million litres of alcohol
Stills	Wash: 1
	Spirit: 1
Main bottling	No age statement, 40%
Nose	Rich vanilla and coconut with a hint of green apple and a tang of citrus zest.
Taste	Sweet vanilla cream, fresh green apple skin and a little mint.
Finish	Fresh, floral zestiness.
Comments	The Lowlands' only triple-distilled malt.
Also try	Glengoyne, Littlemill, Tobermory
Availability	Everywhere
Price	£25–30

Malt	**BLADNOCH**
Pronounced	*BLAAD-noch*
Distillery	Bladnoch
	BLADNOCH
	DG8 9AB
Owner	Coordinated Development Services Ltd
Reception centre	01988 402235
Website	www.bladnoch.co.uk
Established	1817
Status	In production
Water source	River Bladnoch
Malt source	Commercial maltsters
Phenolic content	Unpeated with occasional peated distillations
Casks	Ex-bourbon, refill hogsheads and butts
Annual output	250,000 litres of alcohol
Stills	Wash: 1
	Spirit: 1
Main bottling	8 years old, 46%
Nose	Light, floral, estery.
Taste	Medium-bodied, with citrus zest and floral overtones.
Finish	Refreshing and spicy.
Comments	Fine pre-dinner drinking.
Also try	Aultmore, Bunnahabhain, Loch Lomond
Availability	Specialist retailers and at the distillery
Price	£32 plus

Daftmill Distillery
stillhouse

Malt	**DAFTMILL**
Distillery	Daftmill
	CUPAR
	KY15 5RF
Owner	Cuthbert Family
Reception centre	Guided tours by strict appointment
Website	www.daftmill.com
Established	2005
Status	In production
Water source	Local springs
Malt source	Grown on the farm, malted locally
Phenolic content	Unpeated
Casks	Ex-bourbon and sherry
Annual output	20,000 litres of alcohol
Stills	Wash: 1
	Spirit: 1
Comments	As Daftmill malt is currently maturing in bond, there are no tasting notes.
Availability	Currently not available

Malt	GLENKINCHIE
Distillery	Glenkinchie
	PENCAITLAND
	EH34 5ET
Owner	Diageo
Reception centre	01875 342004
Website	www.malts.com
Established	1837
Status	In production
Water source	Local spring
Malt source	Roseisle Maltings
Phenolic content	Lightly peated
Casks	Ex-bourbon casks
Annual output	2.5 million litres of alcohol
Stills	Wash: 1
	Spirit: 1
Main bottling	12 years old, 43%
Nose	Aromatic, vanilla, cut flowers and beneath, a clean, toasty note. Fresh citrus, lemon cheesecake.
Taste	Light, smooth-bodied. Sweet, becoming flowery, then butter icing, lemon cheesecake and freesias.
Finish	Herbal and drying, a little like pot-pourri.
Comments	Diageo's premier Lowland distillery is well worth visiting.
Also try	Bladnoch, Glen Moray, Auchentoshan
Availability	Widespread
Price	£30 plus

Malt	**INVERLEVEN**
Pronounced	*Inver-LEEV-inn*
Distillery	Inverleven
Established	1938. Closed 1991.
Status	Lost
Main bottling	Independents
Nose	Delicate hint of dry smoke.
Taste	Quite full-bodied, warming, smooth with some wood.
Finish	Long, dry with a nuance of fruit.
Comments	Another lost dram. The distillery plant will be used for the proposed Port Charlotte Distillery on Islay.
Also try	Glengoyne, Auchentoshan, Bladnoch
Availability	Very rare. Specialist retailers
Price	£40 plus

Malt	**KILLYLOCH**
Distillery	Moffat AIRDRIE
Established	1965. Closed 1986. Demolished 1988.
Status	Lost
Main bottling	Independents
Comments	Killyloch was one of the two malts from the Moffat distilling complex in Airdrie which closed in 1985. The other was Glen Flagler. Killyloch production ceased in the late 1960s. Due to its rarity, no tasting notes have been recorded.
Also try	Kinclaith, Littlemill, Auchentoshan
Availability	Very rare. Specialist retailers
Price	£1500 plus

Malt	**KINCLAITH**
Pronounced	*Kin-KLAITH*
Distillery	Kinclaith
Established	1956/7. Dismantled 1976/7.
Status	Lost
Main bottling	Independents
Nose	Light and smoky with a spirit sharpness.
Taste	Full-bodied and smooth.
Finish	Attractive.
Comments	One of Glasgow's lost drams.
Also try	Auchentoshan, Glengoyne, Glen Flagler
Availability	Very rare. Specialist retailers
Price	£650 plus

Malt	**LADYBURN**
Distillery	Ladyburn
Established	1966. Closed 1975.
Status	Lost
Main bottling	Independents
Nose	Dry and floral with an underlying touch of wood.
Taste	Medium-bodied, sweet with citrus, spice and vanilla.
Finish	Long with honey sweetness and oak.
Comments	Ailsa Bay Distillery is now established on the same site as Ladyburn. All independent bottlings usually refer to this malt as 'Ayrshire' for legal reasons.
Also try	Bladnoch, Auchentoshan, Littlemill
Availability	Very rare. Specialist retailers
Price	£130 plus

Malt	**LITTLEMILL**
Distillery	Littlemill
Established	1772. Closed 1984.
Status	Lost
Main bottling	12 years old, 40%
Nose	Light and delicate, dry and fruity.
Taste	Light, mellow-flavoured, slightly cloying.
Finish	Pleasant and warming.
Comments	A lost dram from one of Scotland's oldest distilleries, now no more.
Also try	Auchentoshan, Ladyburn, Bladnoch
Availability	Very rare. Specialist retailers
Price	£25–30

Malt	**ROSEBANK**
Distillery	Rosebank
Website	www.malts.com
Established	c.1840. Closed 1993.
Status	Lost
Main bottling	Rare Malts, Special Releases and independent bottlings
Nose	Sweet fruits and meadow-flower aromas.
Taste	Soft, long and lively. Intensely sweet floweriness, developing sweet, clean lemon flavours; then some spiciness.
Finish	Short, fresh, dry ginger.
Comments	A triple-distilled and much lamented loss to Scotland's malt whiskies.
Also try	Auchentoshan, Glengoyne, Glenkinchie
Availability	Specialist retailers
Price	£44 plus

Malt	**ST MAGDALENE**
Distillery	St Magdalene
Website	www.malts.com
Established	c.1798. Closed 1983. Now converted to residential use.
Status	Lost
Main bottling	Rare Malts and independent bottlings
Nose	Fresh, light, oaky sweetness. Smoky and dry, a real pot pourri of enhancing aromas.
Taste	Sweet at first, developing to a smooth, well balanced dryness with a smoky flavour.
Finish	Slow but ripe.
Comments	Another of Scotland's lost Lowland drams. Also available as Linlithgow.
Also try	Rosebank, Auchentoshan, Bladnoch
Availability	Rare. Specialist retailers
Price	£100 plus

Islay

ISLAY malt whisky is perhaps the most characteristic of all. However, the island's product — traditionally the heaviest and most pungent available — does conceal a few surprises. The Islay style is due to production methods which were developed in concert with the available distilling ingredients in this remote locality. Renowned as the most fertile island in the Hebrides, Islay had three major assets in this regard: a ready source of local bere or barley, inexhaustible amounts of peat and burns running brimful with soft water. Coupled to this was the likelihood that the art of distilling was probably brought to Islay from Ireland by the MacBeatha clan, hereditary physicians to the MacDonalds, the Lords of the Isles until 1493, who gifted them land in the Kilchoman area.

While the urban markets were supplied by mainland distillers in the 18th and 19th centuries, the islanders supplied local markets from stills — both legal and illegal — which were operated from farmyards, bothies in the remote glens above Port Ellen and caves along the precipitous coast of the Oa.

It is impossible to visit Islay and not notice the peat. Crossing the enormous Laggan Moss between Port Ellen and Bowmore the peat banks stretch as far as the eye can see. This fuel was the only means by which the islanders could dry their grain — an essential process not only in distilling, but also for storage during the wet season. By kilning barley it could be kept for longer and the drier the grain was, the less likely it was to go mouldy.

As the grain dried in the peat smoke, it imparted a highly distinctive character which manifested itself when the spirit was finally distilled from it. These flavours are still apparent in most of today's Islay malts and are best experienced by trying Ardbeg, Lagavulin, Laphroaig, Port Ellen, Kilchoman and Octomore (from Bruichladdich). The latter pair are new malts being produced in the traditional Islay style while the first four are all from the Kildalton parish along Islay's southern coast. The other Islays of Bruichladdich,

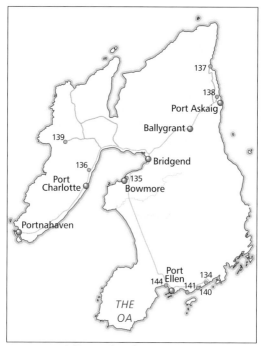

Distillery number refers to page number

Bunnahabhain and Caol Ila display the peaty-smoky accent to a far lesser degree depending on the expression. The core Bruichladdich bottling is unpeated, Bunnahabhain is very lightly peated and Caol Ila is now producing large amounts of entirely unpeated malt. For those new to the world of malt Bunnahabhain is an excellent entrée to the Islays and is a fine aperitif malt.

Islay has become an incredibly popular place for whisky enthusiasts especially at the time of the annual Feis Ile at the end of May (www.theislayfestival.co.uk/whisky.html) but be warned, book well ahead as accommodation goes quickly. Anyone who does venture over to this wonderful island will be struck by the fact that all the Islay distilleries are in coastal locations. The reason? During the mid-to-late 19th century the sea was the 'road' to the mainland markets and all the distilleries were directly accessible by boat so commerce and the provision of supplies such as coal and casks were better facilitated. In contrast the smaller inland farm distilleries fell victim to their more remote locations and gradually closed down. Remnants of some of these are still visible at Octomore above Port Charlotte where the old distillery has been converted into first-class holiday accommodation, Tallant Farm above Bowmore and Lossit Kennels near Bridgend. The surviving distilleries all cater for visitors to Islay and there is a particularly good café at Ardbeg.

Sadly Port Ellen Distillery is now lost with only two symbolic pagoda-topped kilns remaining along with the shore-front warehousing which is still in use today. The Port Ellen Maltings are fully operational and supply most of the malt requirements for the island's distilleries. However the best news over the last decade has been the establishment of Kilchoman Distillery at Rockside Farm, the rebirth of Bruichladdich and the subsequent plans by its owners to build a new distillery at Port Charlotte. Bruichladdich has traditionally produced one of the lighter Islay malts but they are now increasing the range of bottlings to include heavily peated styles such as Octomore and the PC series. The distillery was one of the first to be built from modern concrete in 1880–1 as was its neighbour, Bunnahabhain, which was constructed at the same time.

Across Lochindaal directly opposite Bruichladdich lies Bowmore, which is the perfect base for exploring the island. Just down the Sound of Islay from Bunnahabhain is Caol Ila, which was extensively modernised in 1974 and now possesses views of the Paps of Jura from the still-house that are breathtaking. Caol Ila produces a medium-bodied Islay in unpeated and peated expressions and is now becoming increasingly available. Bowmore also is medium-bodied and one of the most popular Islay malts.

The Islays in general, however, should be approached with great respect since they are that part of the master blender's palette which he uses sparingly to help create the blends which have been the bedrock of the industry for over 150 years.

Malt	ARDBEG
Pronounced	*Aard-BEGG*
Distillery	Ardbeg
	PORT ELLEN
	PA42 7EB
Owner	LVMH
Reception centre	01496 302244
Website	www.ardbeg.com
Established	1815
Status	In production
Water source	Loch Uigeadail
Malt source	Port Ellen Maltings
Phenolic content	55–65 ppm
Casks	First and second refill ex-bourbon with some ex-sherry
Annual output	1 million litres of alcohol
Stills	Wash: 1
	Spirit: 1
Main bottling	10 years old, 46%
Nose	Intense smoky fruit and effervescent peat.
Taste	Tangy lemon and lime and warm creamy cappuccino.
Finish	Long smoky, aniseedy and almondy.
Comments	Resurrected in 1997, this is now one of Scotland's finest malt whiskies.
Also try	Lagavulin, Croftengea, Port Charlotte
Availability	Everywhere
Price	£38

Malt	**BOWMORE**
Pronounced	*Bow-MORE*
Distillery	Bowmore
	BOWMORE
	PA43 7GS
Owner	Suntory
Reception centre	01496 810441
Website	www.bowmore.com
Established	1779
Status	In production
Water source	River Laggan
Malt source	Floor maltings 30% and Simpson's, Berwick-Upon-Tweed — all Scottish malt
Phenolic content	26 ppm
Casks	Ex-bourbon barrels, hogsheads and ex-sherry butts
Annual output	1.46 million litres of alcohol
Stills	Wash: 2
	Spirit: 2
Main bottling	12 years old, 40%
Nose	Subtle notes of lemon and honey bound in a distinctive smokiness.
Taste	Medium-bodied, warming mouthfeel revealing exotic fruits, subtle dark chocolate and peat smoke.
Finish	Lingering with a floral tribute.
Comments	Popular, middle-Islay malt.
Also try	Glen Scotia, Springbank, Highland Park
Availability	Everywhere
Price	£25 plus

Malt	**BRUICHLADDICH**
Pronounced	*Broo-ick-LADD-ay*
Distillery	Bruichladdich
	BRUICHLADDICH
	PA49 7UN
Owner	Murray McDavid Ltd
Reception centre	01496 850190
Website	www.bruichladdich.com
Established	1881
Status	In production
Water source	Bruichladdich Burn
Malt source	50% organic, 25% local, 10% bere, 15% regular from Baird's
Phenolic content	Unpeated
Casks	First fill ex-bourbon, ex-wine and ex-sherry finishes employed
Annual output	800,000 litres of alcohol
Stills	Wash: 2
	Spirit: 3
Main bottling	6 years old, 46%
Nose	Soft red grapes, redcurrant jelly, pomegranate, red apple with syrup, malt and brown-sugar vanilla.
Taste	Malt and oak with wine flavours then red cherry, strawberry and spice.
Finish	Creamy with a snappy coastal crispness.
Comments	Just one of the many expressions available from Islay's most innovative distiller.
Also try	Bowmore, Bunnahabhain, Springbank
Availability	Everywhere
Price	£25–35

Malt	**BUNNAHABHAIN**
Pronounced	*Bonna-HAAV-inn*
Distillery	Bunnahabhain
	PORT ASKAIG
	PA46 7RP
Owner	C L Financial
Reception centre	01496 840646
Website	www.bunnahabhain.com
Established	1881
Status	In production
Water source	Margadale Spring for process and Loch Staoisha for cooling
Malt source	Unpeated from Simpson's, peated malt from Port Ellen Maltings
Phenolic content	1–2 ppm
Casks	Fresh and refill sherry butts and hogsheads; fresh and refill ex-bourbon, refill ex-whisky barrels, butts and hogsheads plus de-charred, re-charred casks
Annual output	2.7 million litres of alcohol
Stills	Wash: 2
	Spirit: 2
Main bottling	12 years old, 40%
Nose	Aromatic with a subtle whiff of smoke.
Taste	Light, slightly nutty with malty sweetness.
Finish	Full-bodied and lingering.
Comments	A fine pre-dinner malt.
Also try	Bruichladdich, Tobermory, Loch Lomond
Availability	Widespread
Price	£25–30

Malt	CAOL ILA
Pronounced	*Cull EEL-ah*
Distillery	Caol Ila
	PORT ASKAIG
	PA46 7RL
Owner	Diageo
Reception centre	01496 302760
Website	www.malts.com
Established	1846
Status	In production
Water source	Loch Nam Ban
Malt source	Port Ellen Maltings
Phenolic content	Unpeated and up to 35 ppm
Casks	Refill ex-bourbon hogsheads
Annual output	3.8 million litres of alcohol
Stills	Wash: 3
	Spirit: 3
Main bottling	12 years old, 43%
Nose	Clean, appetising with subtle citrus fruit and a tiny hint of smoke.
Taste	Firm and smooth-bodied, starts sweetly then yields to a fragrant smokiness.
Finish	Sweet smokiness in the lingering, slightly sour finish.
Comments	The new Lagavulin?
Also try	Talisker, Lagavulin, Kilchoman
Availability	Widespread
Price	£30 plus

Malt	**KILCHOMAN**
Pronounced	*Kill-CHOM-inn*
Distillery	Kilchoman
	BRUICHLADDICH
	PA49 7UT
Owner	Kilchoman Distillery Co Ltd
Reception centre	01496 850011
Website	www.kilchomandistillery.com
Established	2005
Status	In production
Water source	Allt Glean Osmail
Malt source	Floor maltings 30% and Port Ellen Maltings
Phenolic content	45 ppm
Casks	80% first-fill ex-Buffalo Trace bourbon, 20% first-fill ex-Oloroso sherry butts from Miguel Martin
Annual output	100,000 litres of alcohol
Stills	Wash: 1
	Spirit: 1
Main bottling	5 years old, 46%
Nose	Strong, peaty aromas and a complex blend of pear drops, citrus and hints of mango.
Taste	An initial sweetness is followed by peat smoke and mixed fruits.
Finish	Long, clean and refreshing leaving hints of peat-smoke and cloves.
Comments	Still maturing nicely and getting better with the years.
Also try	Croftengea, Ardbeg, Lagavulin
Availability	Specialist retailers
Price	£45 plus

Malt	**LAGAVULIN**
Pronounced	*Laga-VOOL-inn*
Distillery	Lagavulin
	PORT ELLEN
	PA42 7DX
Owner	Diageo
Reception centre	01496 302730
Website	www.malts.com
Established	1816
Status	In production
Water source	Solum Lochs
Malt source	Port Ellen Maltings
Phenolic content	30–35 ppm
Casks	Refill American hogsheads and some refill European wood
Annual output	2.25 million litres of alcohol
Stills	Wash: 2
	Spirit: 2
Main bottling	16 years old, 43%
Nose	Intensely flavoured, peat smoke with iodine and seaweed and a rich, deep sweetness.
Taste	Full-bodied. Rich, dried-fruit sweetness, smoky, intense, peppery smoke at the back.
Finish	Huge, long, warming and peppery with a distinct appetising sweetness.
Comments	One of the great malts and rightly so.
Also try	Ardbeg, Laphroaig, Ledaig
Availability	Everywhere
Price	£40 plus

Malt	**LAPHROAIG**
Pronounced	*La-froyg*
Distillery	Laphroaig
	PORT ELLEN
	PA42 7DU
Owner	Fortune Brands
Reception centre	01496 302496
Website	www.laphroaig.com
Established	1815
Status	In production
Water source	Kilbride Dam, Loch na Beinn Breac
Malt source	Floor maltings 30% and Port Ellen Maltings
Phenolic content	35–40 ppm
Casks	Ex-bourbon
Annual output	2 million litres of alcohol
Stills	Wash: 3
	Spirit: 4
Main bottling	10 years old, 40%
Nose	Medicinal, well-balanced, peaty-smoky. Delightfully pungent.
Taste	Big, peaty flavour. Unmistakeable. Betrays its proximity to the sea.
Finish	Lingering and long. Delightful touch of sweetness.
Comments	The world's favourite Islay malt? Perhaps.
Also try	Lagavulin, Port Ellen, Brora
Availability	Everywhere
Price	£25–30

Malt	OCTOMORE
Pronounced	*Okto-MORE*
Distillery	Bruichladdich
	BRUICHLADDICH
	PA49 7UN
Owner	Murray McDavid Ltd
Reception centre	01496 850190
Website	www.bruichladdich.com
Established	1881
Status	In production
Water source	Bruichladdich Burn
Malt source	50% organic, 25% local, 10% bere, 15% regular from Baird's
Phenolic content	140 ppm
Casks	First fill ex-bourbon, ex-wine and ex-sherry finishes employed
Annual output	800,000 litres of alcohol
Stills	Wash: 2
	Spirit: 3
Main bottling	5 years, 61%
Nose	Peat, bracken, smoky bacon, dry seaweed, pitch, tarry fishnets, then subtle notes of wild flowers and heather.
Taste	Mellow oak, malt, some lemon citrus, heather honey and black pepper.
Finish	Long, lingering with a bourbon endnote.
Comments	The world's most peated malt whisky. Finished in Château Pétrus barrels.
Also try	Croftengea, Ardbeg, Lagavulin
Availability	Specialist retailers
Price	£78 plus

Malt	**PORT CHARLOTTE**
Pronounced	*Port SHARR-lot*
Distillery	Bruichladdich
	BRUICHLADDICH
	PA49 7UN
Owner	Murray McDavid Ltd
Reception centre	01496 850190
Website	www.bruichladdich.com
Established	1881
Status	In production
Water source	Bruichladdich Burn
Malt source	50% organic, 25% local, 10% bere, 15% regular from Baird's
Phenolic content	40 ppm
Casks	First fill ex-bourbon, ex-wine and ex-sherry finishes employed
Annual output	800,000 litres of alcohol
Stills	Wash: 2
	Spirit: 3
Main bottling	8 years old, 60.5%
Nose	Sea spray, peat smoke, spicy pepper, lemon, heather, myrtle, sweet oak and malt.
Taste	Warming peat and sweet oaky Demerara sugar notes.
Finish	Mellow and rich.
Comments	The eighth release of the 2001 vintage, matured in American oak, limited to 30,000 numbered bottles.
Also try	Laphroaig, Kilchoman, Ardbeg
Availability	Specialist retailers
Price	£64 plus

Malt	PORT ELLEN
Distillery	Port Ellen
Website	www.malts.com
Established	1825. Closed 1983. Warehouses and two kilns remain.
Status	Lost
Main bottling	Rare Malts, Special Releases and independent bottlings
Nose	Soft pear fruit and burnt driftwood tar. Traces of shellfish with a hint of herbs.
Taste	Firm and dry, sweet at first then massively smoky then some salt.
Finish	Long, warming with lingering peat smoke.
Comments	Rare and becoming rarer. Prices are spiralling upwards for this fine Islay malt.
Also try	Ardbeg, Laphroaig, Brora
Availability	Rare. Specialist retailers
Price	£125 plus

Campbeltown

THE re-emergence of Glengyle Distillery during the first decade of the new millennium has been great news for the whisky lover. Over 100 years ago, this town was the capital of distilling in Scotland, and Glengyle (established in 1873) was one of 20 active distilleries when Alfred Barnard visited in 1886. The others were Albyn (1830), Ardlussa (1879), Argyll (1844), Benmore (1868), Burnside (1825), Campbeltown (1815), Dalaruan (1824), Dalintober (1832), Glen Nevis (1877), Glenside (1830), Lochead (1824), Kinloch (1823), Kintyre (c.1826), Lochruan (1835), Longrow (1824), Rieclachan (1825), Scotia (1832), Springbank (1828) and Springside (1830).

These operations were a throwback to the days when illicit distilling in the district around the town was rife; between 1797 and 1817 no legal whisky was distilled in this area but after the Excise Act of 1823, distilling in the region largely went legal with 13 distilleries being established within a decade of the new legislation. For the next century or so, Campbeltown boomed and the town prospered until the industry eventually collapsed in the 1920s. The reasons? Primarily demand dropped for Campbeltown whisky as the blenders gravitated towards Speyside and Islay for their component malts. There was a great deal of over-production as well, and many distillery closures were followed by years of trustees and liquidators trying to sell off stock that few wanted. Only Springbank and Glen Scotia survived this disastrous period.

It would be unwise, however, to forget Campbeltown's contribution to distilling in Scotland. It remains one of the six *appellations* and its malt had a distinctive style which in its heyday resembled the Islay malts. Today, Longrow perhaps comes closest to the old Campbeltown product. Modern-day Springbank is a very elegant whisky which is distilled two-and-half times in a complex arrangement of charging one wash still and two low wines stills. This distillery is unique on many fronts. It is the only distillery to malt all its own barley (and Glengyle's), it bottles its own products, it is still in family hands and it produces three malts of varying character. Its survival is a tribute to the quality of these malt whiskies.

Despite its relative remoteness at the heel of Kintyre, the trip to Campbeltown can be undertaken as part of a tour to Islay and there is plenty of accommodation in the town. With its rich heritage in whisky-making it seems strange that the town does not celebrate it more. Perhaps it feels slightly ashamed of how great it once was, and is now embarrassed by what it has lost? Certainly a whisky trail could be created which would take visitors on a bracing walk around the main locations with a final saunter up the Gallowhill to look over the town in the same way as the photographers of the late-Victorian and Edwardian periods did when they recorded the full extent of the town's commercial might. Perhaps it might happen yet?

Malt	GLEN SCOTIA
Pronounced	*Glen SKOASH-ah*
Distillery	Glen Scotia
	CAMPBELTOWN
	PA28 6DS
Owner	Loch Lomond Distillery Ltd
Website	www.lochlomonddistillery.com
Established	1832
Status	In production
Water source	Crosshill Loch and borehole aquifers
Malt source	Greencore Maltings of Buckie
Phenolic content	Unpeated and peated
Casks	Ex-bourbon barrels
Annual output	1 million litres of alcohol
Stills	Wash: 1
	Spirit: 1
Main bottling	12 years old, 40%
Nose	Apples, honey and a hint of seaweed.
Taste	Light, sweet, tangy with a hint of smoke.
Finish	Dry with subtle wood and smoke notes.
Comments	A Campbeltown survivor and much underrated.
Also try	Springbank, Oban, Bunnahabhain
Availability	Specialist retailers
Price	£20 plus

Malt	**HAZELBURN**
Distillery	Springbank
	CAMPBELTOWN
	PA28 6ET
Owner	J & A Mitchell & Co Ltd
Reception centre	By appointment. 01586 551710
Website	www.springbankwhisky.com/hazelburn/
Established	1828
Status	In production
Water source	Crosshill Loch
Malt source	Floor maltings
Phenolic content	Unpeated
Casks	Ex-bourbon, ex-sherry and refill hogsheads
Annual output	750,000 litres of alcohol
Stills	Wash: 1
	Spirit: 2
Main bottling	8 years old, 46%
Nose	Light and delicate with subtle nuances of raspberry coulis, shortbread and sherbet. Sweet vanilla, malt and white oak are also in evidence.
Taste	Elegantly sweet and malty. Loads of vanilla flavour combines well with toasty oak notes leading to a spicey aftertaste.
Finish	A slightly peppery finish to a refined and elegant triple-distilled dram.
Comments	One of the three malts produced by Springbank Distillery.
Also try	Auchentoshan, Rosebank, Glen Scotia
Availability	Specialist retailers
Price	£30 plus

Malt	**KILKERRAN**
Pronounced	*Kil-KERR-an*
Distillery	Glengyle
	CAMPBELTOWN
	PA28 6EX
Owner	J & A Mitchell & Co Ltd
Website	www.kilkerran.com
Established	1872. Closed 1925–2004.
Status	In production
Water source	Crosshill Loch
Malt source	Springbank Distillery floor maltings
Phenolic content	8–10 ppm
Casks	Ex-bourbon, ex-sherry and refill hogsheads
Annual output	750,000 litres of alcohol
Stills	Wash: 1
	Spirit: 1
Main bottling	6 years old, 46%
Nose	An initial burst of perfume leads to a sweet, fruity and eventually spicy aroma.
Taste	Cloves, with a fruity sweetness. Already lively, zesty and full of flavour.
Finish	Sweet with lingering vanilla.
Comments	12,000 bottles will be released annually until 2016 when the 12 year-old will be ready.
Also try	Springbank, Glen Scotia, Bunnahabhain
Availability	Specialist retailers
Price	£30 plus

Malt	**LONGROW**
Distillery	Springbank
	CAMPBELTOWN
	PA28 6ET
Owner	J & A Mitchell & Co Ltd
Reception centre	By appointment. 01586 551710
Website	www.springbankwhisky.com
Established	1828
Status	In production
Water source	Crosshill Loch
Malt source	Floor maltings
Phenolic content	Up to 50 ppm
Casks	Ex-bourbon, ex-sherry and refill hogsheads
Annual output	750,000 litres of alcohol
Stills	Wash: 1
	Spirit: 2
Main bottling	10 years old, 46%
Nose	Sweet vanilla with dried fruit, straw, gentle smoke. Phenolic.
Taste	Wet wool with oak, phenolic with tar and salt.
Finish	Sweet peat lingers, mouthfilling, moreish.
Comments	A throwback to the old-fashioned Campbeltown style.
Also try	Caol Ila, Brora, Ardmore
Availability	Specialist retailers
Price	£30 plus

Malt	SPRINGBANK
Distillery	Springbank
	CAMPBELTOWN
	PA28 6ET
Owner	J & A Mitchell & Co Ltd
Reception centre	By appointment. 01586 551710
Website	www.sprinbankwhisky.com
Established	1828
Status	In production
Water source	Crosshill Loch
Malt source	Floor maltings
Phenolic content	8–10 ppm
Casks	Ex-bourbon, ex-sherry and refill hogsheads
Annual output	750,000 litres of alcohol
Stills	Wash: 1
	Spirit: 2
Main bottling	10 years old, 46%
Nose	Orchard pears with a hint of peat, vanilla and malt.
Taste	Malt, oak, spice, nutmeg and cinnamon, vanilla essence.
Finish	Sweet with a lingering salty tingle.
Comments	Two-and-half-times distilled. The class act from Campbeltown.
Also try	Kilkerran, Glen Scotia, Bunnahabhain
Availability	Widespread
Price	£25–30

The Islands

THERE is another addition to the portfolio of Island distilleries now that the Abhainn Dearg (pronounced *AA-vin JERR-ick*) micro-distillery is in production on the Isle of Lewis although product samples are scarce and so we have not listed any further details here. This brings the total number of Island distilleries to seven, stretching from Arran in the Firth of Clyde to Scapa and Highland Park in Orkney. Arran has come of age in the last decade and its 10-year-old expression is now their core malt in the UK market while they continue to make big inroads into foreign markets such as Norway where it is now the second top-selling malt.

The longer established Island brands seem to be in good health with Diageo's Talisker maintaining its position as one of the most successful award-winning single malts. Similarly Highland Park's reputation around the world remains as high as ever and its close neighbour Scapa is now more widely available. Tobermory is enjoying a much more stable existence on Mull than previously and is part of Burn Stewart Distillers portfolio. Under master blender Richard Paterson's direction Isle of Jura has expanded its range of expressions and is now one of the most widely available in the UK.

On the other side of the coin, there now seems little chance of the proposed Shetland Distillery coming to fruition and the other planned distillery on Barra is currently no further forward. Despite this the heritage of distilling in the islands is well recorded and was something on which the island clan chiefs placed great value. However, heavy drinking and the subsequent social problems it created was a big problem in the clan society of the Hebrides and in 1609 the import of strong wines and aquavitae was banned while home-brewing and distillation for private use was allowed to continue. That craft was the bedrock from which the industry evolved out of the crofts and farmyards and into the multi-million pound businesses that now exist throughout the islands. In a sense, Abhainn

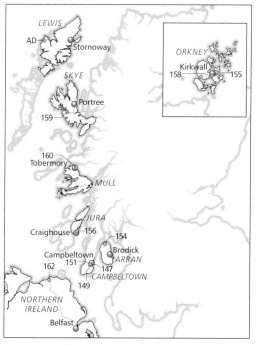

Distillery number refers to page number.
AD = Abhainn Dearg

Dearg, is testament to this tradition as it seems to have literally appeared from nowhere.

The Island malt whisky styles are variable and display distillery characteristics from the heather-honey signature of Highland Park to the maritime pepper finish of Talisker. Along the way you will discover Jura's Highland flavour, Tobermory's light peatiness and Arran's floral freshness. The region, if it can be described as such, is geographically huge so it is best dealt with by visitors as a series of side-trips when in the area nearest to the island you are interested in.

Malt	ARRAN
Distillery	Arran
	LOCHRANZA
	KA27 8HJ
Owner	Isle of Arran Distillers Ltd
Reception centre	01770 830264
Website	www.arranwhisky.com
Established	1995
Status	In production
Water source	Eason Biorach
Malt source	Commercial maltsters
Phenolic content	Unpeated but a peated expression is bottled at 20 ppp
Casks	Ex-bourbon barrels, ex-sherry hogsheads, butts and puncheons
Annual output	250,000 litres of alcohol
Stills	Wash: 1
	Spirit: 1
Main bottling	10 years old, 46%
Nose	Rich vanilla sweetness then exotic fruits. Complex yet harmonious.
Taste	Soft and sweet, mouth-coating with a hint of cinnamon. Citrus notes against a background of sweet oak.
Finish	Long, lingering with a golden syrup feel.
Comments	One of Scotland's newest distilleries, beautifully situated.
Also try	Speyside, Glen Grant, Tobermory
Availability	Widespread
Price	£25–30

Malt	**HIGHLAND PARK**
Distillery	Highland Park
	KIRKWALL
	KW15 1SU
Owner	Edrington Group
Reception centre	01856 873107
Website	www.highlandpark.co.uk
Established	1798
Status	In production
Water source	Cattie Maggie's Spring
Malt source	Floor maltings 20% and Simpson's, Berwick-Upon-Tweed
Phenolic content	20–30 ppm
Casks	Refill ex-sherry Spanish and American oak and small proportion of ex-bourbon
Annual output	2.75 million litres of alcohol
Stills	Wash: 2
	Spirit: 2
Main bottling	12 years old, 40% and 43%
Nose	Heather-honey sweetness with some peaty smokiness.
Taste	Rounded smoky sweetness with a full malt mouthfeel.
Finish	Teasing, heathery with subtle smoke. Absolutely delicious.
Comments	A gem of a malt.
Also try	Springbank, Scapa, Bowmore
Availability	Everywhere
Price	£23 plus

Malt	JURA
Pronounced	*JOO-ra*
Distillery	Jura
	Isle of Jura
	PA60 7XT
Owner	United Spirits
Reception centre	01496 820420
Website	www.isleofjura.com
Established	c.1810. Rebuilt 1960–3.
Status	In production
Water source	Loch A'Bhaile Mhargaidh
Malt source	Commercial maltsters
Phenolic content	Unpeated
Casks	First and refill ex-bourbon with some ex-sherry casks
Annual output	2.2 million litres of alcohol
Stills	Wash: 2
	Spirit: 2
Main bottling	10 years old, 40%
Nose	American white oak, cinnamon, crushed pear and apple. Almond, pine wood and lemon grass with subtle hints of gorse and sea spray.
Taste	Gentle oak flavours with caramel, soft liquorice, flashes of roasted coffee beans and crusty wholemeal bread.
Finish	Long and lingering.
Comments	Bottled in a wide range of expressions.
Also try	Glen Garioch, Bunnahabhain, Oban
Availability	Everywhere
Price	£25 plus

Malt	**LEDAIG**
Pronounced	*Led-CHIG*
Distillery	Tobermory
	Isle of Mull
	PA75 6NR
Owner	C L Financial
Reception centre	01688 302645
Website	www.burnstewartdistillers.com
Established	1798
Status	In production
Water source	Gearr Abhainn
Malt source	Unpeated malt from mainland maltsters, peated malt from Port Ellen Maltings
Phenolic content	35–45 ppm
Casks	Fresh and refill ex-bourbon, sherry butts and hogsheads, refill barrels, butts and hogsheads plus de-charred, re-charred casks
Annual output	1 million litres of alcohol
Stills	Wash: 2
	Spirit: 2
Main bottling	10 years old, 40%
Nose	Pungent with sweet tar, creosote and wood smoke. Hints of liquorice, antiseptic and charred leather.
Taste	Sweet, medicinal with spicy pepper. Smoky with a subtle salt maltiness.
Finish	A spicy, smoked pepper finale.
Comments	A striking contrast to Tobermory.
Also try	Ardbeg, Laphroaig, Croftengea
Availability	Widespread
Price	£25–30

Malt	**SCAPA**
Pronounced	*SKAA-pa*
Distillery	Scapa
	KIRKWALL
	KW15 1SE
Owner	Pernod Ricard
Website	www.scapamalt.com
Established	1824
Status	In production
Water source	Lingro Burn
Malt source	Kilgours of Kirkcaldy
Phenolic content	Unpeated
Casks	Ex-bourbon casks
Annual output	1 million litres of alcohol
Stills	Wash: 1
	Spirit: 1
Main bottling	16 years old, 40%
Nose	Heavy, butterscotch sweetness, dried fruits, subtle hints of orange.
Taste	Smooth and full-bodied. Perfectly balanced wild honey and heather, delicate spices.
Finish	Very rich and long with a distinct dry aftertaste.
Comments	Scapa uses a reworked Lomond still in its process. Remains in the shadow of its neighbour Highland Park.
Also try	Highland Park. Cragganmore, Strathisla
Availability	Specialist retailers
Price	£50

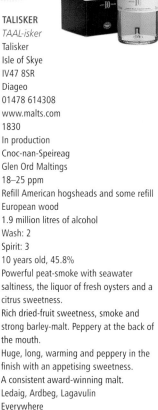

Malt	**TALISKER**
Pronounced	*TAAL-isker*
Distillery	Talisker
	Isle of Skye
	IV47 8SR
Owner	Diageo
Reception centre	01478 614308
Website	www.malts.com
Established	1830
Status	In production
Water source	Cnoc-nan-Speireag
Malt source	Glen Ord Maltings
Phenolic content	18–25 ppm
Casks	Refill American hogsheads and some refill European wood
Annual output	1.9 million litres of alcohol
Stills	Wash: 2
	Spirit: 3
Main bottling	10 years old, 45.8%
Nose	Powerful peat-smoke with seawater saltiness, the liquor of fresh oysters and a citrus sweetness.
Taste	Rich dried-fruit sweetness, smoke and strong barley-malt. Peppery at the back of the mouth.
Finish	Huge, long, warming and peppery in the finish with an appetising sweetness.
Comments	A consistent award-winning malt.
Also try	Ledaig, Ardbeg, Lagavulin
Availability	Everywhere
Price	£25 plus

Malt	**TOBERMORY**
Pronounced	*Tober-MORE-ay*
Distillery	Tobermory
	Isle of Mull
	PA75 6NR
Owner	C L Financial
Reception centre	01688 302645
Website	www.tobermorymalt.com
Established	1798
Status	In production
Water source	Gearr Abhainn
Malt source	Unpeated malt from mainland maltsters, peated malt from Port Ellen Maltings
Phenolic content	1–2 ppm
Casks	Fresh and refill ex-bourbon, sherry butts and hogsheads, refill barrels, butts and hogsheads plus de-charred, re-charred casks
Annual output	1 million litres of alcohol
Stills	Wash: 2
	Spirit: 2
Main bottling	10 years old, 40%
Nose	Fresh, lightly peated, smokey.
Taste	Medium-dry with a smooth and fruity tang.
Finish	Well-rounded and rich.
Comments	Lighter than its Ledaig stablemate.
Also try	Arran, Glengoyne, Mannochmore
Availability	Widespread
Price	£25–30

Northern Ireland

DISTILLING used to be prevalent in this region but it suffered, as it did throughout the rest of Ireland, during the 1920s and is now only active at Bushmills. Distilleries such as Avoniel, Connswater, Royal Irish, Comber, Abbey Street, Coleraine and Limavady have all come and gone and the whiskeys they produced are now unobtainable. Bushmills is perhaps the most fitting survivor as it claims to be the oldest licensed distillery in the world, dating back to 1608 although the recently resurrected Kilbeggan Distillery in County Westmeath disputes this as the Bushmills' date refers to the granting of a licence by King James I and VI to the area of Antrim within the Ulster plantation that he had created. Kilbeggan's licence of 1757 relates directly to the site of the distillery.

Irish whiskey differs from its Scots neighbours in that it is usually distilled from a mash of malted and unmalted barley and is also distilled three times. The result is a lighter-bodied spirit akin to some of its close Lowland counterparts. However, Bushmills is a malt whiskey distillery producing expressions at 10, 16 and 21 years of age; not the traditional practice in Ireland. It is also the signature whiskey in the premium Black Bush blend and its trade blend Bushmills Original.

The distillery is very well set up to cater for visitors and over 100,000 of them come to Bushmills every year. During Pernod Ricard's negotiations to buy Allied Domecq in 2005, Bushmills found itself a pawn in a corporate chess game which led to it being sold by Pernod Ricard to Diageo for £200 million so long as Diageo did not bid for Allied Domecq. The distillery is an essential stopping-off place on any tour along the beautiful coast of County Antrim.

Malt	BUSHMILLS
Distillery	Old Bushmills
	BUSHMILLS
	BT57 8XH
Owner	Diageo
Reception centre	028 2073 3218
Website	www.bushmills.com
Established	1608
Status	In production
Water source	St Columb's Rill
Malt source	Commercial maltsters
Phenolic content	Unpeated
Casks	Ex-bourbon and sherry with some port pipes
Annual output	3 million litres of alcohol
Stills	Wash: 4
	Spirit: 5
Main bottling	10 years old, 40%
Nose	Fresh and zesty. Honey and ripe fruit.
Taste	Soft. Vanilla, milk chocolate and toasted wood.
Finish	Crisp and clean, gently drying.
Comments	Our closest malt whiskey neighbour, a mere 27 km from Islay.
Also try	Bladnoch, Bowmore, Bruichladdich
Availability	Everywhere
Price	£25–30

4. Blended Malt Scotch

THIS category used to be known as 'vatted' malt Scotch whisky but following the 2009 regulations, blended malt whisky is what it is going to be known as from now on. So why do producers bottle a mixture of malts in this fashion? In essence it is a throwback to the mid-1850s when a change in the law allowed producers to vat whiskies while still in bond. At that time the search for a more generic, palatable whisky was in full flow in order to appeal to a much wider market than the single malt (or 'self') whiskies that were then the only real option available to the drinking public. Andrew Usher then created the first vatted malt with Usher's Old Vatted Glenlivet. However, he soon realised that by combining patent-still grain whisky with a selection of malts, his aim to satisfy the desires of the public were more readily achieved and for less cost. Blended whisky became the norm and vatted malts were to remain a curiosity on the sidelines from then on.

In order to acquire a taste for single malts it could be argued that the blended malts are an intermediate step up from blended Scotch, but they are notoriously difficult to create as they lack the large canvas that is grain whisky on which the master blender is able to craft a blended Scotch from the constituent malts on his palette.

They are available however and can be found on the supermarket shelves in the shape of 15-year-old Johnnie Walker Green Label and William Grant & Sons' Monkey Shoulder. Given that stock management is at the core of a distiller's ability to maintain the supply of brands, it might be that more blended malts with no age statements will appear on the market as they draw from much younger stocks than they would normally do. In truth though, this category will remain small in relation to blended Scotch whisky, but it is worth venturing into nonetheless.

Whisky	BIG PEAT
Owner	Douglas Laing & Co Ltd
Main bottling	No age statement, 46%
Nose	Peaty with sweet notes of honey and toffee.
Taste	Sweet with lingering peat and a slightly floral note in the background.
Finish	Long, lingering and robust with some chocolate.
Comments	A blend of malts including Ardbeg, Caol Ila, Bowmore and Port Ellen.
Also try	Ardbeg, Caol Ila, Islay Mist
Availability	Widespread
Price	£30
Website	www.douglaslaingwhisky.com

Whisky	JOHNNIE WALKER GREEN LABEL
Owner	Diageo
Main bottling	15 years old, 40%
Nose	Complex, malty, sea brine and peat.
Taste	Cloying, summer fruits, pine, cut grass. Sophisticated and rewarding.
Finish	Long, lingering and warming.
Comments	A fine blended malt Scotch made from Talisker, Caol Ila, Cragganmore and Linkwood.
Also try	Monkey Shoulder, Spice Tree
Availability	Widespread
Price	£29
Website	www.johnniewalker.com

Whisky	MONKEY SHOULDER
Owner	William Grant & Sons Ltd
Main bottling	No age statement, 40%
Nose	Floral, citrus,peaches, apricots. Honey, oak and vanilla.
Taste	Vanilla, brown sugar, creamy toffee, oak. Cinnamon and nutmeg hints.
Finish	Smooth, lingering, sweet.
Comments	A blend of Glenfiddich, Balvenie and Kininvie malts.
Also try	Johnnie Walker Green Label, Spice Tree
Availability	Everywhere
Price	£23
Website	www.williamgrant.com

Whisky	SPICE TREE
Owner	Compass Box
Main bottling	No age statement, 46%
Nose	Cloves, ginger, cinnamon, nutmeg and vanilla.
Taste	Full, round and sweet with spice and vanilla.
Finish	Long and lingering.
Comments	A blend of aged Northern Highland malts. Matured in American oak then custom-made barrels using heavily toasted new French oak heads from the Vosges forest.
Also try	Johnnie Walker Green Label, Monkey Shoulder
Availability	Specialist retailers
Price	£35
Website	www.compassboxwhisky.com

5. Single Grain Scotch

IF blended Scotch malts are a rarity then single grain Scotch whiskies are even more so. The only proprietary brand on the market is Diageo's Cameron Brig with all the other bottlings coming from independent bottlers who have secured stocks from Scotland's six active grain distilleries as well as four of the other five distilleries that have been decommissioned in the past 40 years.

The result of this is that the single largest component whisky in the annual output of Scotch whisky is barely represented at the retail end of the spectrum. From a cultural perspective this is not surprising as grain whisky has always been considered the sleeping partner in the make up of a Scotch blend, but this ignores the fact that grain spirit must have 'an aroma and taste derived from the raw materials used in, and the method of, its production.' That requirement is legal in order for it to be termed Scotch grain whisky. It might be high in strength, but neutral and flavourless it can never be.

Grain whiskies also vary in the way they are produced as some distillers employ the basic two-column set up (see page 16) producing a fairly full and oily distillate whereas others have multiple columns giving a cleaner and lighter spirit. The result is that Scotland's six grain distilleries produce differing grain whiskies with distinct distillery character.

The magic in grain whisky really begins with the maturation process. Predominately this will be in first-fill ex-bourbon casks which will give vanilla and coconut notes as well as mellowing the spirit which can be metallic when new. Over time the grain whisky is sweetened until, when fully mature, it gently coats the mouth with a luxurious vanilla character. Indeed most grains take well to being much longer in cask than malts and some of the vintage independent bottlings can stand up to many single malts. They may be few in number, but they are worth the effort to track down and try, although your pockets might have to be deep.

Whisky	INVERGORDON
Distillery	Invergordon
	INVERGORDON
	IV18 0HP
Owner	United Spirits
Established	1961
Status	In production
Water source	Loch Glas
Cereals source	Wheat and barley from the East of Scotland
Casks	Ex-bourbon
Annual output	36 million litres of alcohol
Main bottling	Independents
Nose	Sweet, toffee sauce on vanilla ice cream. Hint of pancakes and white chocolate.
Taste	Chewy Caramac bars, melted butter, lemon sorbet and home-made fudge.
Finish	Brittle toffee and slightly burnt shortbread, Some spicy notes.
Comments	A great example of how well single grains age.
Also try	Strathclyde, Cambus, Loch Lomond
Availability	Rare. Specialist retailers
Price	£50 plus

Whisky	**LOCH LOMOND**
Distillery	Loch Lomond
	ALEXANDRIA
	G83 0TL
Owner	Loch Lomond Distillery Ltd
Website	www.lochlomonddistillery.com
Established	1966
Status	In production
Water source	Borehole aquifers and Loch Lomond
Cereals source	Commercial grain dealers
Casks	Ex-bourbon casks
Annual output	4 million litres of alcohol
Main bottling	5 years old, 45%
Nose	Soft and sweet.
Taste	Light, sweet and buttery with vanilla tones.
Finish	Refreshing and clean.
Comments	Only available direct from the distillery.
Also try	Strathclyde, Port Dundas, Garnheath
Availability	Specialist retailers and at the distillery
Price	£25 plus

Whisky	CAMERON BRIG
Distillery	Cameron Bridge
	WINDYGATES
	KY8 5RL
Owner	Diageo
Established	1824
Status	In production
Water source	Borehole aquifers
Cereals source	Wheat from East Coast of Scotland, malt from Burghead Maltings
Phenolic content	Unpeated
Casks	First fill and refill ex-bourbon
Annual output	100 million litres of alcohol
Main bottling	No age statement, 40%
Nose	Slight, with some spice, vanilla and a hint of oak.
Taste	Some dried fruit, citrus with a hint of sherry-oak and caramel.
Finish	Smooth and mouth-coating with oak nuances.
Comments	The only single grain Scotch bottled by its proprietors.
Also try	Cambus, Carsebridge, Strathclyde
Availability	Specialist retailers
Price	£15 plus

Whisky	GIRVAN
Distillery	Girvan
	GIRVAN
	KA26 9PY
Owner	William Grant & Sons Ltd
Website	www.wiliamgrant.com
Established	1964
Status	In production
Water source	Penwhapple Loch
Cereals source	Home-grown wheat and malted barley
Casks	Ex-bourbon
Annual output	70 million litres of alcohol
Main bottling	1964, 48%
Comments	No tasting notes available.
Also try	Strathclyde, Cambus, Loch Lomond
Availability	Very rare. Specialist retailers
Price	£290 plus

Whisky	**NORTH BRITISH**
Distillery	North British
	EDINBURGH
	EH11 2PX
Owner	Diageo and Edrington Group
Website	www.northbritish.co.uk
Established	1887
Status	In production
Water source	Pentland Hills
Cereals source	Maltings on site with 25% of cereal mash as malted barley, the remainder is maize
Casks	Ex-bourbon
Annual output	64 million litres of alcohol
Main bottling	Independents
Nose	Banana fritters, toffee and cream.
Taste	Ripe creamy bananas, rhubarb and custard.
Finish	Smooth and silky with the distinct toffee notes lingering.
Comments	Edinburgh's last remaining distillery.
Also try	Loch Lomond, Cambus, Carsebridge
Availability	Specialist retailers
Price	£20 plus

Whisky	STRATHCLYDE
Pronounced	*Strath-CLYDE*
Distillery	Strathclyde
	GLASGOW
	G5 0ND
Owner	Pernod Ricard
Established	1927
Status	In production
Water source	Mains water from Loch Katrine
Cereals source	Local commercial maltsters and grain suppliers
Casks	Ex-bourbon
Annual output	39 million litres of alcohol
Main bottling	Independents
Nose	Heather honey and creamy toffee.
Taste	Smooth a bit fruity with vanilla fudge.
Finish	Oily, long and creamy.
Comments	Glasgow's last remaining distillery.
Also try	Port Dundas, Cambus, Garnheath
Availability	Very rare. Specialist retailers
Price	£90 plus

Whisky	**CAMBUS**
Distillery	Cambus
Established	1806. Closed 1993. Warehouses remain.
Status	Lost
Main bottling	Independents
Comments	No tasting notes available.
Also try	Cameron Brig, Strathclyde, Carsebridge
Availability	Very rare. Specialist retailers
Price	£45 plus

Whisky	**CARSEBRIDGE**
Distillery	Carsebridge
Established	1799. Closed 1983. Warehouses remain.
Status	Lost
Main bottling	Independents
Nose	Rich, warm toffee, vanilla builds up and also a touch of spice.
Taste	Oily, very chewy. Digestive biscuits with melted butter. Marzipan and green olives.
Finish	Initial toffee notes fade, then grassier notes emerge. Ends with lingering plums.
Comments	A reminder of Clackmannan's great distilling heritage.
Also try	Cambus, Cameron Brig, Garnheath
Availability	Very rare. Specialist retailers
Price	£65 plus

Whisky	GARNHEATH
Distillery	Moffat
Established	1965. Closed 1986. Demolished 1988.
Status	Lost
Main bottling	Independents
Comments	Another extinct grain whisky. No tasting notes available.
Also try	Cambus, Strathclyde, Carsebridge
Availability	Very rare. Specialist retailers
Price	£100 plus

Whisky	PORT DUNDAS
Distillery	Port Dundas
Established	1810. Closed 2010.
Status	Lost
Main bottling	Independents
Nose	Fresh oak, vanilla, cinnamon spice, butter fudge.
Taste	Chewy with oak and spice.
Finish	Creamy vanilla, long-lasting.
Comments	Port Dundas ceased distilling in March 2010. Its capacity has been taken up by Cameron Bridge.
Also try	Strathclyde, Cambus, Carsebridge
Availability	Very rare. Specialist retailers
Price	£80 plus

6. Blended Grain Scotch

NOW we are down to the rarest of the rare, although this category could well expand if there is sufficient demand. Of the big players only the Edrington Group has ventured here with The Snow Grouse, a whisky that they suggest should be chilled before consumption. Unlike a chilled vodka, this type of Scotch has been influenced by the wood in which the constituent grains have matured, so the experience is more rewarding. The other whisky we are looking at is Compass Box's Hedonism which is an altogether more complex (and expensive) beast. You can find the three constituent single grain whiskies from which it is made in the preceding chapter.

This category would probably not exist had it not been for Compass Box's founder, American John Glaser, who recognised that the single grain whiskies produced in Scotland were worth exploring, blending and then bottling. The result in Hedonism is extraordinary and will take you on a unique taste adventure. It will be interesting to see where this category goes in the coming years but there is no doubt that as the appreciation of grain whiskies increases, there should be an increasing availability of product for the consumer.

And you thought Scotch whisky was all about malts and blends?

Whisky	HEDONISM
Owner	Compass Box
Main bottling	No age statement, 43%
Nose	Elegant with vanilla to the fore.
Taste	Vanilla, pastry cream, toffee and coconut.
Finish	Silky, creamy oak.
Comments	Grain whisky sourced from Cameron Bridge, Carsebridge and Cambus, aged between 14 and 29 years and matured in first-fill American oak barrels and rejuvenated American oak hogsheads.
Also try	The Snow Grouse, Cameron Brig
Availability	Specialist retailers
Price	£47
Website	www.compassboxwhisky.com

Whisky	THE SNOW GROUSE
Owner	Edrington Group
Main bottling	No age statement, 40%
Nose	Soft creamy vanilla, cloudy honey, nutmeg and lightly oaky. After chilling the creamy vanilla comes to the fore.
Taste	Smooth and sweet vanilla fudge. After chilling the mouthfeel is viscous, smooth vanilla with no sense of alcohol fire.
Finish	Sweet and lingering. After chilling the aftertaste is warming with a lingering sweetness.
Comments	The first mainstream blended grain Scotch to be issued by one of the big distillers.
Also try	Hedonism, Cameron Brig
Availability	Specialist retailers
Price	£19
Website	www.thefamousgrouse.com

7. Blended Scotch

TO cover all the available Scotch blends would mean writing another couple of books on this category. The ones we are listing here are a selection of some of the blends found just about everywhere, such as in supermarkets and High Street wine and spirit merchants. However, you will doubtless come across many other Scotch blends, especially in duty free and while on holiday abroad. Many of these will be unfamiliar to UK residents. The reason is that distillers have built up some brands exclusively in export markets and have UK brands for the home market as well. We have included one such brand from Bacardi, William Lawson, which is ubiquitous in Europe but almost impossible to source in Britain. As this is a beginners' guide we have not selected blended whiskies from the higher-priced premium (also known as deluxe) category, as these are rarer in number than the common blends, but worth trying nonetheless.

Blends are commonly categorised by price with unaged bottlings generally available between £10 and £20, and the premium, aged blends like Chivas Regal coming in above the £20 mark. These blends contain a higher proportion of malts than the unaged blends (although the non-premium Teacher's Highland Cream is the exception to this rule with a malt content of 45%). It goes without saying that the grain whiskies used in a premium blend are also aged and of a very high quality.

Although the expectation of most newcomers to Scotch whisky might be that a lot of blends are likely to be quite similar, the art of the master blender assures that there is plenty of variety in style and character from light and creamy to full-bodied and smoky over a wide price range. In short, blended Scotch whiskies offer something for everyone … which is exactly what Andrew Usher envisaged when he created the first blended Scotch over 150 years ago.

Whisky	**BALLANTINE'S**
Owner	Pernod Ricard
Main bottling	No age statement, 40%
Nose	Soft, elegant heather honey with a hint of spice.
Taste	Well-balanced subtle flavours with tones of milk chocolate, red apple and vanilla.
Finish	Refreshing, floral and rounded.
Comments	A very popular blend overseas.
Also try	William Lawson, Whyte & Mackay, Teacher's
Availability	Widespread
Price	£18
Website	www.ballantines.com

Whisky	**BELL'S ORIGINAL**
Owner	Diageo
Main bottling	No age statement, 40%
Nose	Soft, gentle with hints of barley. Quite floral.
Taste	Smooth, medium-bodied with cereal, oak and spice overtones.
Finish	Quite short but pleasant with a trace of smoke and some fruitcake.
Comments	The age statement has gone. Has some of the quality?
Also try	Teacher's, The Famous Grouse, Whyte & Mackay
Availability	Everywhere
Price	£15
Website	www.bells.co.uk

Whisky	**BLACK BOTTLE**
Owner	C L Financial
Main bottling	No age statement, 40%
Nose	Fresh and fruity with hints of peat.
Taste	Full with slight sweetness followed by a delightful smoky flavour.
Finish	Long and warming with an interesting, smoky, Islay character.
Comments	Now revitalised.
Also try	Islay Mist, Isle of Skye, The Black Grouse
Availability	Everywhere
Price	£15
Website	www.blackbottle.com

Whisky	**DEWAR'S WHITE LABEL**
Owner	Bacardi
Main bottling	No age statement, 40%
Nose	Sweet heather and honey with notes of vanilla, coffee, liquorice, citrus and unripened pear.
Taste	Medium-bodied, soft vanilla with honey and floral notes. Well-rounded.
Finish	Medium finish, slightly dry with lingering heather-honey overtones and a faint touch of smoke.
Comments	America's favourite blended Scotch.
Also try	Teacher's, J&B, Ballantine's
Availability	Widespread
Price	£16
Website	www.dewarswow.com

Whisky	GRANT'S FAMILY RESERVE
Owner	William Grant & Sons Ltd
Main bottling	No age statement, 40%
Nose	Clean with hints of banana.
Taste	Complex banana and vanilla sweetness balancing sharper malty tones.
Finish	Medium and satisfying.
Comments	Formerly branded as Standfast, a distinctive bottle shape makes this blend stand out.
Also try	Whyte & Mackay, Bell's, The Famous Grouse
Availability	Everywhere
Price	£15
Website	www.williamgrant.com

Whisky	HIGH COMMISSIONER
Owner	Loch Lomond Distillery Ltd
Main bottling	No age statement, 40%
Nose	Young but fresh, light with some malt.
Taste	Traces of malt against a light, fresh and slightly floral background.
Finish	Finishes quickly but is pleasant enough.
Comments	A good mixer Scotch and one of the highest-selling value blends available.
Also try	The Famous Grouse, Bell's, Scottish Leader
Availability	Everywhere
Price	£10
Website	www.lochlomonddistillery.com

Whisky	**ISLAY MIST**
Pronounced	*EYE-la Mist*
Owner	MacDuff International Limited
Main bottling	No age statement, 40%
Nose	Salty, seaweed, peat and smoke.
Taste	Less peat than on the nose. Oily with some grassy hints and light oak.
Finish	Perfectly balanced peat, oak and vanilla.
Comments	Created for Lord Margadale's coming of age in 1922 and based heavily on Laphroaig.
Also try	Black Bottle, Isle of Skye, The Black Grouse
Availability	Specialist retailers
Price	£18
Website	www.islaymist.com

Whisky	**ISLE OF SKYE**
Owner	Ian Macleod & Co Ltd
Main bottling	8 years old, 40%
Nose	A hint of smoke and peat.
Taste	Smooth and sweet with some honey and vanilla overtones.
Finish	Long and lingering.
Comments	A fine aged blend based largely on Island and Speyside malts.
Also try	Black Bottle, Islay Mist, The Black Grouse
Availability	Widespread
Price	£15
Website	www.ianmacleod.com

Whisky	J&B
Owner	Diageo
Main bottling	No age statement, 40%
Nose	Fruity and nutty with some citrus, fruit and barley.
Taste	Medium-bodied, well balanced. Smooth with fruit nuances.
Finish	A trace of oak and spice. Fairly short.
Comments	Claims to be Europe's favourite blend and the 'ultimate party whisky' with a make-up consisting of 42 whiskies.
Also try	William Lawson, Dewar's, Ballantine's
Availability	Widespread
Price	£18
Website	www.jbscotch.com

Whisky	JOHNNIE WALKER RED LABEL
Owner	Diageo
Main bottling	No age statement, 40%
Nose	Fresh, fruity, spicy and smoky.
Taste	Vibrant, fresh with sweet, with peaty, vanilla, spicy and malty overtones.
Finish	Warm, lingering and smoky.
Comments	The world's most popular blended Scotch whisky.
Also try	Ballantine's, Whyte & Mackay, Teacher's Highland Cream
Availability	Everywhere
Price	£16
Website	www.johnniewalker.com

Whisky	**SCOTTISH LEADER**
Owner	C L Financial
Main bottling	No age statement, 40%
Nose	Lightly peated.
Taste	Sweet to start leading to a honey richness. Full-bodied.
Finish	Long, dry with a lingering hint of peat.
Comments	An increasingly popular blend.
Also try	Bell's, Whyte & Mackay, The Famous Grouse
Availability	Widespread
Price	£15
Website	www.scottishleader.co.uk

Whisky	**TEACHER'S HIGHLAND CREAM**
Owner	Fortune Brands
Main bottling	No age statement, 40%
Nose	Malty with a peat-smoke tang. Then apples, pears and heavy honey.
Taste	Full and rich. Slowly fades to a silky roundness.
Finish	Well balanced with a clean, busy fullness that lingers.
Comments	One of the highest malt contents in any non-aged blend, 45%.
Also try	Whyte & Mackay, Ballantine's, Johnnie Walker Red Label
Availability	Everywhere
Price	£14
Website	www.teacherswhisky.com

Whisky	**THE BLACK GROUSE**
Owner	Edrington Group
Main bottling	No age statement, 40%
Nose	Hints of peat smoke and a touch of spice.
Taste	Smooth, rich with a hint of peat smoke. Well-rounded.
Finish	Long, smoky and aromatic.
Comments	A welcome addition to The Famouse Grouse family.
Also try	Black Bottle, Islay Mist, Isle of Skye
Availability	Everywhere
Price	£16
Website	www.thefamousgrouse.com

Whisky	**THE FAMOUS GROUSE**
Owner	Edrington Group
Main bottling	No age statement, 40%
Nose	Slightly smoky, with a hint of citrus.
Taste	Well-balanced with some floral notes, touches of smoke, cereal, citrus and a hint of vanilla.
Finish	Long and clean.
Comments	Scotland's best-selling blended whisky.
Also try	Bell's, Whyte & Mackay, Scottish Leader
Availability	Everywhere
Price	£14
Website	www.thefamousgrouse.com

Whisky	**WHYTE & MACKAY SPECIAL**
Owner	United Spirits
Main bottling	No age statement, 40%
Nose	Full, round, soft. Well balanced.
Taste	Good mouthfeel, warming with hints of honeyed soft fruits.
Finish	Long and lingering.
Comments	Very popular in the West of Scotland and beautifully presented.
Also try	Bell's, Grant's Family Reserve, Teacher's
Availability	Everywhere
Price	£14
Website	www.whyteandmackay.com

Whisky	**WILLIAM LAWSON**
Owner	Bacardi
Main bottling	No age statement, 40%
Nose	Fruity with notes of ice cream and apple crumble.
Taste	Medium-bodied. Well balanced mixture of toasted biscuits and sweet caramel.
Finish	Medium, slightly dry and oaky.
Comments	Exclusively available at the Scotch Whisky Experience, Edinburgh. Very popular in Duty Free and export markets.
Also try	Ballantine's, Johnnie Walker Red Label, Teacher's
Availability	See Comments
Price	£15

Index of Distilleries and Brands